NEW YORK

OFF THE BEATEN PATH™

FOURTH EDITION

WILLIAM G. AND KAY SCHELLER

A Voyager Book

The Globe Pequot Press

Old Saybrook, Connecticut

Library of Congress Cataloging-in-Publication Data

Scheller, William.
    New York : off the beaten path / William G. and Kay Scheller. —
4th ed.
        p.   cm.
    Includes index.
    ISBN 0-7627-0070-X
    1. New York (State)—Guidebooks. I. Scheller, Kay. II. Title.
F117.3.S35   1997   96-40448
917.4704'43—dc21   CIP

Manufactured in the United States of America
Fourth Edition/First Printing

To Sally—always there for us,
always ready to go.

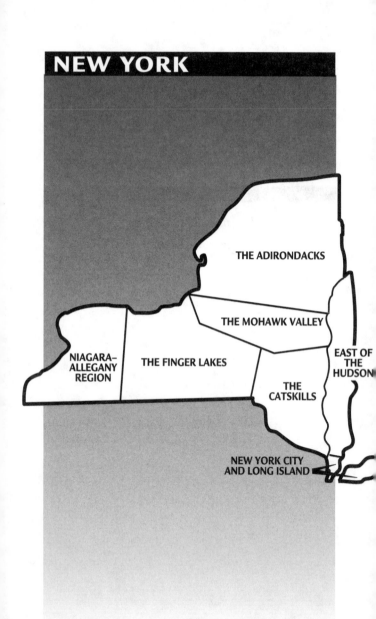

NEW YORK

THE ADIRONDACKS

THE MOHAWK VALLEY

NIAGARA–
ALLEGANY
REGION

THE FINGER LAKES

EAST OF
THE
HUDSON

THE
CATSKILLS

NEW YORK CITY
AND LONG ISLAND

CONTENTS

INTRODUCTION

Back in 1986, when we researched the first edition of *New York: Off the Beaten Path*, the challenge seemed to be to find enough places that would meet the title's criterion. After all, the paths that run between Montauk and Niagara, between Binghamton and Massena, are among the most heavily beaten in the United States. Could there by any stones left unturned in such a place?

Of course there were. And over the course of ten years and three revisions, we've been able to find pathways ever more untrammeled and obscure. After a decade of combing the backstreets and two-lane blacktops of the Empire State, we've seen this book evolve in ways that have allowed us to delete many better-known attractions and replace them with the kind of places you aren't likely to find in any other guide. Here are butterflies and buffalos, grape pies and glassblowers, places famous for making kazoos and carousels, and a kaleidoscope as big as a silo (actually, it *is* a silo). Along the way we've turned up the kind of restaurants and overnight accommodations favored by aficionados of the less-traveled roads. There are more eateries and lodging places than ever in these pages, and not one of them serves portion-controlled meals or offers a room identical to one you've stayed in on an interstate in Nebraska.

New York occupies a unique position in American history, a position between that of the small, densely settled New England states and the western expanses left untamed well into the nineteenth century. With the exception of the Dutch settlements at New Amsterdam and along the Hudson Valley, New York remained a virtual frontier until the late 1700s. When it was settled, the newcomers were not colonists from abroad but in many cases migrating New Englanders, men and women setting the pattern for the next hundred years of westward expansion. New York thus became a transitional place between old, coastal America and the horizons of the West.

More than that, the future "Empire State" became a staging area for the people, ideas, and physical changes that would transform the United States in the nineteenth century. Its position between the harbors of the Atlantic coast and the Great Lakes assured early prominence in the development of canals and later railroads. Its vast resources made it an industrial power, while its size and fertility guaranteed its importance as a farm state. It began its growth early enough to create an infrastructure of small towns connected by back roads, rivers, and canals and remained vigorous in a modern era conducive to the rise of great cities along busy trunkline railroads. All the while, the state's geographical diversity allowed its different regions to assume varied and distinct personalities.

The spiritual and intellectual atmosphere in New York was no less responsive to change. This is where the quietist Shakers played out much of their experiment in plain living, where Washington Irving proclaimed a native American literature, where the artists of the Hudson River School painted American nature as it had never been painted before, and where Elbert

Hubbard helped introduce the Arts and Crafts movement to the United States.

This book is about the rich legacy of tangible associations that all of this activity has left behind. New York is crammed as are few other states with the homes, libraries, and workshops of famous individuals, with battlefields and the remnants of historic canals, with museums chronicling pursuits as divergent as horse racing, gunsmithing, and wine making. In a place where people have done just about everything, here are reminders of just about everything they've ever done—and since this isn't merely a history book, it will introduce you to plenty of New Yorkers who are still hard at work building their state and filling it with interesting things.

Within each of the regional chapters of this book, the order of individual listings has been determined geographically, as explained in the chapter introductions. Few readers will be proceeding dutifully from site to site, so no attempt has been made to provide detailed linking directions. Still, it's nice to know what's near what if a slightly longer drive would make visits to several destinations possible.

Once again—for the fourth time in ten years—we're off to New York State. An especially enlightening journey is promised to all those New Englanders who thought the world ended at Lake Champlain; to Manhattanites for whom "upstate" is Yonkers; to Midwesterners, Westerners, and Southerners who think they hold the patents on small towns and open country; and to travelers from abroad who would like to learn a little more about how America came to be what it is.

The rest of you are from New York State, and you know what you've been hiding.

Note to Readers: In the course of writing this book, we were careful to obtain the most recent available information regarding schedules and admission fees at each attraction described. All of these details were accurate at the time the book went to press; however, hours of operation and prices are always subject to change. Just to be sure, use the telephone numbers provided to check these details before each visit.

The prices and rates listed in this guide-book were confirmed at press time. We recommend, however, that you call establishments before traveling to obtain current information.

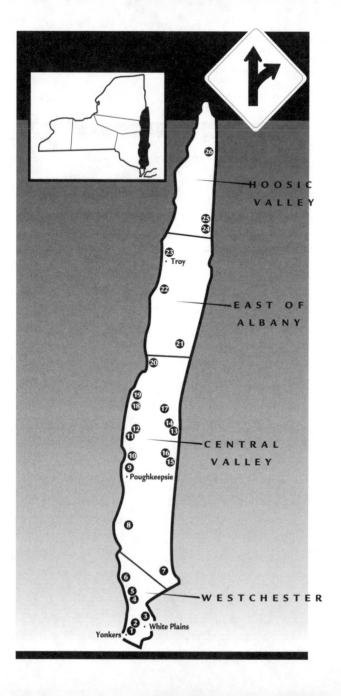

HOOSIC
VALLEY

26

25
24

23
• Troy

22

EAST OF
ALBANY

21

20

19
18

17

14
13

12
11

CENTRAL
VALLEY

10
9
9
• Poughkeepsie

16
15

8

7

WESTCHESTER

6
5
4

3
2   • White Plains
1
Yonkers

EAST OF THE HUDSON

1. Hudson River Museum of Westchester
2. Philipse Manor Hall
3. Donald M. Kendall Sculpture Gardens
4. Lyndhurst
5. Sunnyside
6. Ossining Urban Cultural Park Visitor Center
7. Southeast Museum
8. Van Wyck Homestead
9. Locust Grove
10. The Culinary Institute of America
11. Mills Mansion
12. Belvedere Mansion
13. Troutbeck
14. Cascade Mountain Vineyards
15. Old Drovers Inn
16. Wing's Castle
17. Hudson Valley Raptor Center
18. Kaatsban International Dance Center
19. Clermont
20. Olana
21. Shaker Museum and Library
22. Crailo
23. The Junior Museum
24. Mt. Nebo Gallery
25. New Skete Communities
26. Log Village Grist Mill

EAST OF THE HUDSON

The first of our seven New York State regions begins in the crowded bedroom communities of Westchester County and extends northward into the western foothills of the Berkshires and the Green Mountains. Hilly itself throughout, it encompasses the eastern slopes of one of the most beautiful river valleys in the world. Anyone in need of convincing should drive north along the length of the Taconic State Parkway, which runs through the high country midway between the Hudson and the Connecticut and Massachusetts borders. Along with the more easterly and meandering State Route 22, the Taconic makes for a nice backdoor entry into New England and an even more scenic trip than the more heavily traveled New York State Thruway on the other side of the river. Many of the attractions described in this chapter, however, are clustered along the river itself and are mainly accessible via U.S. Route 9, once the carriage road that connected the feudal estates of Old Dutch New York. Franklin D. Roosevelt's Hyde Park and the sumptuous Vanderbilt estate are two of the valley's best-known latter-day country seats; in this chapter, though, we'll concentrate on less publicized homesteads and other points of interest. The orientation is from south to north.

WESTCHESTER COUNTY

Just beyond the New York City limits, in Yonkers, the ◆ **Hudson River Museum of Westchester** occupies the magnificent 1876 Glenview Mansion, enhanced by a recent addition designed to provide exhibition space and a planetarium. As the preeminent cultural institution of Westchester County and the lower Hudson Valley, the museum's resources reflect the natural, social, and artistic history of the area.

A visit to the Hudson River Museum includes a walk through the four meticulously restored rooms on the first floor of the mansion itself. You'll hardly find a better introduction to the short-lived but influential phase of Victorian taste known as the Eastlake style, marked by precise geometric carving and ornamentation—the traceries in the Persian carpets almost seem to be echoed in the furniture and ceiling details.

Aside from the furnishings and personal objects that relate to the period when the Trevor family lived in the mansion, the museum's collections have grown to include impressive holdings of Hudson River landscape paintings, including works by Jasper Cropsey and Albert Bierstadt.

In contrast to the period settings and historical emphases of the older parts of the museum, the state-of-the-art Andrus Planetarium features the Zeiss M1015 star projector, the only one of its kind in the Northeast. A contemporary orientation is also furthered by as many as thirty special art, science, and history exhibitions each year, centered on the work of American artists of the nineteenth and twentieth centuries. There are Summer Sounds Dance Concerts in July and a Victorian Holiday celebration each December.

The Hudson River Museum of Westchester, 511 Warburton Avenue, Yonkers 10701, (914) 963-4550, is open Wednesday, Thursday, and Saturday, 10:00 A.M. to 5:00 P.M.; Sunday, noon to 5:00 P.M.; and Friday, 10:00 A.M. to 9:00 P.M. Admission to the museum galleries is $3.00 for adults; $1.50 for senior citizens and children under 12. Admission to the planetarium is $4.00 for adults, $2.00 for senior citizens, and $2.00 for children under 12. There is a free planetarium star show Friday at 7:00 P.M.

Hundreds of years before Glenview Mansion was built, the Philipse family assembled a Westchester estate that makes Glenview's 27 acres seem puny by comparison. Frederick Philipse I came to what was then New Amsterdam in the 1650s and began using his sharp trader's instincts. By the 1690s his lands had grown into a huge estate, comprised in part of a 52,500-acre tract that encompassed one-third of what is now Westchester County.

In 1716 Philipse's grandson, Frederick Philipse II, assumed the title of Lord of the Manor of Philipsborough, greatly enlarged the cottage built by his grandfather, and used ◆**Philipse Manor Hall** as a summer residence. Colonel Frederick Philipse (III) rebuilt and further enlarged the Georgian manor house, planted elaborate gardens, and imported the finest furnishings for the hall. His tenure as Lord of the Manor ended when he decided to side with the Tory cause at the beginning of the American Revolution.

Confiscated along with the rest of its owner's properties after the war, Philipse Manor Hall was auctioned by the state of New York and passed through the hands of a succession of owners until 1908 when the state bought the property back. The state has since maintained the mansion as a museum of history, art, and architecture. Home to the finest papier-mâché rococo ceiling in the United States, inside and out it remains one of the most perfectly preserved examples of Georgian style in the Northeast.

Philipse Manor Hall State Historic Site, 29 Warburton Avenue, P. O. Box 496, Yonkers 10702, (914) 965-4027, is open Wednesday and Thursday from 11:00 A.M. to 2:00 P.M. Weekend hours vary, so call before visiting. Admission is free. Group tours are available by appointment.

Donald M. Kendall, former chairman of the board and chief executive officer of Pepsi Co., Inc., had a dream that extended far beyond soft drinks. He wanted to create a garden whose atmosphere of stability, creativity, and experimentation would reflect his vision of the company. In 1965 he began collecting sculptures; today more than forty works by major twentieth-century artists are displayed on 168 acres of magnificent gardens—many created by internationally renowned designers Russell Page and François Goffinet, who picked up where Mr. Page left off.

Alexander Calder, Jean Dubuffet, Marino Marini, Alberto Giacometti, Auguste Rodin, Henry Moore, and Louise Nevelson are just a few of the artists whose works are displayed in the ◈ **Donald M. Kendall Sculpture Gardens.** Mr. Kendall's artistic vision has truly been realized.

The Donald M. Kendall Sculpture Gardens, Pepsico World Headquarters, 700 Anderson Hill Road, Purchase 10577, (914) 253-2900, is open daily, year-round from 9:00 A.M. to 5:00 P.M. There is no admission fee.

In 1838 the great Gothic Revival architect Alexander Jackson Davis designed ◆**Lyndhurst.** Overlooking the broad expanse of the Tappan Zee from the east, this beautiful stone mansion and its landscaped grounds, built for former New York City mayor William Paulding, represented the full American flowering of the neo-Gothic aesthetic that had been sweeping England since the closing years of the eighteenth century.

Lyndhurst is unusual among American properties of its size and grandeur in having remained under private ownership for nearly a century and a quarter. Paulding and his son owned the estate until 1864, when it was purchased by a wealthy New York merchant named George Merritt. Merritt employed Davis to enlarge the house and to add its landmark tower; he also constructed a large greenhouse and several outbuildings. The greatest legacy of his stewardship, however, was the commencement of an ambitious program to develop an English-inspired romantic landscape to complement the Gothic architecture of the main house.

One of the most notorious of America's railroad robber barons, Jay Gould, acquired Lyndhurst in 1880 and maintained it as a country estate. Upon his death in 1892, Lyndhurst became the property of his oldest daughter, Helen, who left it in turn to her younger sister Anna, duchess of Talleyrand-Perigord, in 1938. The duchess died in 1961, with instructions that the estate become the property of the National Trust for Historic Preservation.

Lyndhurst

Lunch is served in the historic Carriage House from May through October.

Lyndhurst, Route 9 just south of the Tappan Zee Bridge (635 South Broadway), Tarrytown 10591, (914) 631–4481, is open May through October, Tuesday through Sunday, 10:00 A.M. to 5:00 P.M., and November through April, Saturday and Sunday, 10:00 A.M. to 5:00 P.M. Open on Monday holidays. Closed Thanksgiving, Christmas, and New Year's. Admission $7.00 for adults, $6.00 for senior citizens, and $3.00 for children 6 to 16.

Far less imposing than Lyndhurst but a good deal homier, ◆ **Sunnyside** stands just to the south in Tarrytown and offers a fascinating glimpse of the last twenty-four years of its owner, Washington Irving.

Irving described his country retreat as "a little old-fashioned stone mansion, all made up of gable ends, and as full of angles and corners as an old cocked hat." Not surprising for the man who wrote *The Legend of Sleepy Hollow, Rip Van Winkle,* and *Diedrich Knickerbocker's History of New York,* Sunnyside is a step-gabled, Dutch Colonial affair, ivied with time and possessed of more than a little whimsy.

Washington Irving spent two periods of retirement at Sunnyside—the years 1836–42 and the last thirteen years of his life, 1846–59. It was here that he wrote *Astoria,* his account of the Pacific Northwest, as well as *The Crayon Miscellany, Wolfert's Roost,* and *The Life of George Washington.* Here, too, the author entertained such visitors as Oliver Wendell Holmes, William Makepeace Thackeray, and Louis Napoleon III. In the time not taken up with work and hospitality, he planned his own orchards, flower gardens, and arborways. These survive to this day, as do favorite Irving possessions such as the writing desk and piano on view in the house.

Sunnyside, West Sunnyside Lane (1 mile south of the Tappan Zee Bridge on Route 9), Tarrytown 10591, (914) 591–8763, is open daily 10:00 A.M. to 5:00 P.M. from March through December except Tuesday and major holidays. The last tour of the day leaves at 4:00 P.M. Admission is $7.00 for adults, $6.00 for seniors, and $4.00 for children ages 6 to 17. A grounds pass is available for $4.00.

One of the area's newest luxury lodgings is the **Castle at Tarrytown,** a Norman-style mansion built between 1900 and 1910 on ten acres of land overlooking the Hudson River. Surrounded by a stone wall and a magnificent arboretum, the castle features a 40-foot Grand Room with a vaulted ceiling, stained glass windows, and a musicians' balcony. One of the dining rooms has paneling taken from a house outside Paris that was given by France's Louis XIV to James II of England after his removal from the throne in 1688. The castle is at 400 Benedict Avenue in Tarrytown 10591, (914) 631-1980. Call for rates.

There are two wonderful old churches in Sleepy Hollow, which prior to a recent name change was known as North Tarrytown. The **Old Dutch Church of Sleepy Hollow** on Route 9 (914-631-1123), built in 1685, is still heated by a woodstove. Washington Irving's *Legend of Sleepy Hollow* is read in the church during Halloween season. Mass is celebrated Sunday at 10:00 A.M. the second week of June through the first week of September. Tours are given from Memorial Day through October Sunday from 2:00 to 4:00 P.M. and Monday through Thursday from 1:00 to 5:00 P.M. or by appointment. Call for holiday schedules. Donations are accepted.

The tiny **Union Church of Pocantico Hills** on Route 448 (914-631-8200 or 800-448-4007) has a magnificent collection of stained glass windows by Henri Matisse and Marc Chagall, which were commissioned by the Rockefeller family. It's open daily except Tuesday from March through December: weekdays, 11:00 A.M. to 5:00 P.M.; Saturday, 10:00 A.M. to 5:00 P.M.; and Sunday, 2:00 to 5:00 P.M. There's a suggested donation of $3.00.

The menu at the lovely **Crabtree's Kittle House Restaurant and Country Inn** changes daily, but the food, ambience, and service remain consistently superb. Guests can choose a cold salad or hot appetizer, with offerings such as wild salmon gravlax, grilled quail salad, or wild black trumpet mushroom soup. Entrees might include loin of free range lamb; a portobello mushroom, spinach, and red pepper gâteau; or filet mignon. For many, dessert is the high point of a meal in this 1790 mansion, with fanciful confections such as a poached pear under spun sugar or a delicious warm pecan pie. *Wine Spectator Magazine* awarded the restaurant its "Grand Award of Excellence" for having one of the most outstanding restaurant wine lists in the world—more than 30,000 bottles and 1,300 selections.

Crabtree's Kittle House Restaurant and Country Inn, 11 Kittle Road, Chappaqua 10514, (914) 666-8044, has twelve guest rooms. Lunch is served weekdays, dinner nightly, and a Sunday brunch from noon to 2:30 P.M. Reservations are recommended any time, but mandatory on weekends.

In 1826 the State of New York built Sing Sing prison, in Ossining, using convict labor. The prison became famous when "Father" Pat O'Brien walked "gangster" Jimmy Cagney "the last mile" to its electric chair in the movie *Angels with Dirty Faces*. Today a replica of the chair is part of a fascinating exhibition at ⊕ **Ossining Urban Cultural Park Visitor Center.** Divided into two themes, "Down the River: The Old Croton Aqueduct" and "Up the River: Sing Sing Prison," the first part focuses on the construction of the city's aqueduct, historic downtown buildings, and the prison. The second part includes weapons made by prisoners and replicas of an 1825 and a present-day cell.

The Ossining Urban Cultural Park Visitor Center, 95 Broadway, Ossining 10562, (914) 941–3189, is open daily, except Sunday, from 10:00 A.M. to 4:00 P.M. Admission is free.

Peekskill is home to more than seventy artists who work in a variety of mediums. Many of them host **Open Artist Studio Tours** the third Saturday of each month. If you're visiting between mid-June through October, stop at the **Peekskill Farmer's Market** on Bank Street. For information contact The Peekskill/Cortlandt Chamber of Commerce, One South Division Street, Peekskill 10566, (914) 737–3600.

Another important figure of the early Republic, political rather than literary, made his country home to the northeast at Katonah. This was John Jay, whom George Washington appointed to be the first chief justice of the United States and who, with Alexander Hamilton and James Madison, was an author of the *Federalist Papers.* Jay retired to the farmhouse now known as the **John Jay Homestead** in 1801, after nearly three decades of public service, and lived here until his death in 1829.

His son William and his grandson John Jay II lived at the old family homestead, as did John II's son, Col. William Jay II, a Civil War officer of the Union Army. The last Jay to live at the Katonah estate was Eleanor Jay Iselin, the colonel's daughter. After her death in 1953, the property was purchased by Westchester County and turned over to the state of New York as a state historic site.

Having survived so long in the Jay family, the John Jay Homestead is still well stocked with furnishings and associated items that date back to the days when the great patriot lived here. Sixty acres of John Jay's original 900-acre farm are part of the state historic site.

The John Jay Homestead State Historic Site, Route 22, Katonah 10536, (914) 232–5651, is open May through December. From Memorial Day to Labor Day the hours are Wednesday through Saturday, 10:00 A.M. to 5:00 P.M.; Sunday, noon to 5:00 P.M. Call for off-season hours. The last tour enters the mansion at 4:00 P.M. Group tours are by advance reservation. There is a fee of $3.00 for adults, $2.00 for seniors, and $1.00 for children.

In 1907 financier J. P. Morgan built a stone-and-brick Tudor mansion on a hillside overlooking the Hudson River Valley for his friend and minister, William S. Rainsford. The mansion was privately owned until 1973, when it was restored and reborn as a French restaurant called **Le Chateau.** Today, with its dogwood-lined approach, patio and gardens, richly paneled rooms, and elegantly set tables, the restaurant affords patrons the opportunity to enjoy a rapidly diminishing phenomenon—a true dining experience. At Le Chateau, classic French food is prepared and presented in a grand style that matches the atmosphere in which it is served.

Among the house specialties at Le Chateau are grilled shrimp salad with an orange sauce, sea scallops and spinach wrapped in filo with lobster sauce, bouillabaisse, and rack of lamb with a crust of parsley and fresh herbs in rosemary sauce. Elegant desserts include a chocolate Kahlua terrine served with a crème Anglaise and espresso sauce and crème brûlé (caramelized custard). A fixed-price menu is available for $48; a three-course a la carte dinner averages $47.

Le Chateau, Route 35 at the junction of Route 123, South Salem 10590, (914) 533-6631, serves dinner Tuesday, Wednesday, and Thursday from 6:00 to 9:30 P.M.; Friday and Saturday from 6:00 to 10:00 P.M.; and Sunday from 2:00 to 9:00 P.M. Reservations are a must, and jackets are required.

Muscoot Farms is an agricultural holdout in the rapidy suburbanizing Westchester landscape. The early 1900s, 777-acre working farm has a twenty-three-room main house, barns and outbuildings, antique equipment, a large demonstration vegetable garden, and lots of animals. Weekends are a busy time; in addition to hayrides, agricultural programs cover topics such as sheepshearing, harvesting, and beekeeping. There's also a full roster of seasonal festivals. The farm, on Route 100 in Somers 10589, (914) 232-7118, is open daily, 10:00 A.M. to 6:00 P.M. from Memorial Day to Labor Day and 10:00 A.M. to 4:00 P.M. the rest of the year. Donations are welcome.

CENTRAL VALLEY

It takes an interesting region to supply the wherewithal for an interesting regional museum, and Brewster in southern Putnam County has done a good job of filling the bill for the ◆ **Southeast Museum.** The town has been the center of a diverse number of enterprises, including mining, railroading, circuses, and even the manufacture of condensed milk. Reminders of these phases of local history are on exhibit at the museum, which is housed in the 1896 Old Town Hall of Southeast, although the area is commonly referred to as Brewster, for the family that rose to prominence in the 1840s and 1850s.

The first settlers came about 1725. For more than one hundred years, their main pursuits were agriculture and modest cottage industries. In the middle-nineteenth century, Brewster's economic horizons expanded through the arrival of the Harlem Railroad, which became part of Commodore Vanderbilt's vast New York Central system, and the Putnam Line Railroad, a division of the New York and New Haven Line. Railroad days in Brewster are represented at the museum by the artifacts in the David McLane collection.

Brewster was also winter quarters for a number of circuses in the past century. Many of these small local enterprises were later consolidated by P. T. Barnum, who hailed from just across the state line in Connecticut. This most colorful aspect of Brewster's past is recalled in the museum's collection of early American circus memorabilia.

The Southeast Museum, 67 Main Street, Brewster 10509, (914) 279-7500, is open Wednesday, Saturday, and Sunday from noon to 4:00 P.M. and closed on legal holidays. Suggested donation is $2.00.

Your six-course meal at **HARROLDS,** in Stormville, might begin with veal galantine served with Cumberland sauce, followed by onion soup with Emmenthaler cheese. You might then move on to salad with country herb dressing, an entree of roasted duck with blackberry sauce on a bed of wild rice pilaf (and a basket of fruit with a glass of port), and then crown your meal with an ethereal linzer torte. Or you might opt for one of the other choices on the nightly menu, which is wheeled on a blackboard to your table. As you would expect of a restaurant that has earned *Mobil Travel Guide*'s five-star rating for the eighteenth consecutive year, everything will be deliciously prepared, artfully presented, and graciously served. HARROLDS is housed in a large, timbered, 200-year-old cottage with a big stone hearth, brass chandeliers, and a candlelit patio. The custom-built wine house across the way stores more than 250 different wines—most under $30. Harrold Boerger is general manager of the restaurant; his wife, Eva Durrschmidt Boerger, is presiding chef. They work together to ensure diners a splendid gastronomic experience.

HARROLDS, Route 25, Stormville 12582, (914) 878-6595, serves dinner Wednesday to Friday from 6:00 to 9:00 P.M. There are two seatings on Saturday, 5:30 P.M. and 9:30 P.M. Reservations are a must, jackets are required, and credit cards are not accepted. The six-course, fixed-price meal is $60 per person, not including wine. A three-course dinner for $35 per person is served Wednesday and Thursday.

Not all of the Hudson Valley landowners were well-to-do. Most were burghers of a far more modest stamp. The legacy of the life led by one such family is preserved in the ◆ **Van Wyck Homestead,** east of the river in Fishkill. The house was begun in 1732 by Cornelius Van Wyck, who had purchased his nearly 1,000 acres of land from an earlier 85,000-acre Dutchess County estate, and was completed in the

1750s with the construction of the West Wing. For all the land its owners possessed, the homestead is nevertheless a modest affair, a typical Dutch country farmhouse.

Like so many other farmhouses, the Van Wyck Homestead might have been forgotten by history had it not played a part in the American Revolution. Located as it was along the strategic route between New York City and the Champlain Valley, the house was requisitioned by the Continental Army to serve as headquarters for General Israel Putnam. Fishkill served as an important supply depot for General Washington's northern forces from 1776 to 1783. Military trials were held at the house; one such event was reputedly the source used by James Fenimore Cooper for an incident in his novel *The Spy*.

Another factor leading to the homestead's preservation was its having reverted back to the Van Wyck family after the revolution ended. Descendants of its builder lived here for more than 150 years. Today it is operated by the Fishkill Historical Society as a museum of colonial life in the Hudson Valley. The house features a working colonial kitchen fireplace with a beehive oven, which is used during special events. An interesting sidelight is the exhibit of revolutionary war artifacts unearthed in the vicinity during archaeological digs sponsored by the society.

The Van Wyck Homestead, Snook Road (near the intersection of Routes 9 and 84), Fishkill 12524, (914) 896–9560, is open May through October on Sunday from 1:00 to 5:00 P.M. and by appointment. There is an admission charge of $2.00. Bus tours are welcome, and a group rate is offered. Special events include September and holiday craft fairs, a June midsummer festival, and a St. Nicholas Day holiday tour.

Husband and wife team Frank and Michele Nola and their staff create magnificent meals at **The Inn at Osborne Hill.** With appetizers such as duck confit quesadilla and escargot ravioli, entrees like rack of lamb with minted crust and couscous, and prof-iteroles for dessert, the restaurant has earned a reputa-tion as one of Dutchess County's finest. The restau-rant, at 150 Osborne Hill Road, Fishkill 12524, (914) 897–3055, is open for lunch weekdays and dinner nightly except Sunday.

Lewis Country Farms, a 16-acre farm with restored 1861 barns (complete with silo, original post-and-beam ceiling supports, and fieldstone walls) is an all-season kids' stop and shopping mecca.

There are live farm animals for petting, a life-size animated band, antique wagons and sleighs, and spe-cial weekend events. There's a flower shop, a gift shop, a farmers' market selling locally grown produce, an old-fashioned country butcher, freshly baked goods and homemade fudge, a greenhouse and garden cen-ter, and a year-round Christmas shop. And when you get hungry, the folks at Lewis Country Farms will serve up homemade soups and chili, sandwiches, and a heaping salad bar.

Lewis Country Farms, Overlook and DeGarmo roads, Poughkeepsie 12603, (914) 452–7650, is open daily.

In 1847 Samuel F. B. Morse, inventor of the tele-graph and Morse code, purchased 100 acres of land

and a seventeen-year-old Georgian house. With the help of his friend, architect Alexander Jackson Davis, he transformed the original structure into a Tuscan-style villa. Today, ✢ **Locust Grove,** a unique combination of nature preserve, historic gardens, landscaped lawns, vistas, and architecture, is one of the most handsome of the Hudson River estates. In 1963 it became the first in the valley to be designated a National Historic Landmark.

Thirty years after Morse's death, his family sold the property to the Young family, who preserved it essentially as it had been in Morse's time, until 1975, when the estate was bequeathed to a trust "for the enjoyment, visitation, and enlightenment of the public."

Original family furnishings of the Youngs and the Morses are exhibited in period room settings and include rare Duncan Phyfe and Chippendale pieces. Paintings include works by Mr. Morse—a fine painter in his own right—as well as by artists such as George Inness. There's also a rare bound collection of *Birds of America* by J. J. Audubon. A replica of "the invention of the century" is on exhibit in the Morse Room.

Locust Grove, 370 South Road (Route 9), Poughkeepsie 12601, (914) 454-4500, is open daily May through October, from 10:00 A.M. to 4:00 P.M., with tours on Tuesday by appointment only. November, December, March, and April it's open daily 10:00 A.M. to 4:00 P.M. by appointment. Admission is $4.00 for adults, $3.50 for seniors, and $1.00 for children over 6. There is no fee to walk the grounds.

You're now in ✢ **The Culinary Institute of America** country. Founded in 1946, it's the oldest culinary college in the United States and the only residential college in the world devoted entirely to culinary education. And the public is invited to sample the fare from any or all of its four student-staffed restaurants on the 150-acre Hyde Park campus.

St. Andrew's Cafe features casual, well-balanced dining, attractively presented, with dishes ranging from wood-fired pizza to beef tenderloin to apple strudel. The restaurant is open Monday through Friday. Lunch is served from 11:30 A.M. to 1:00 P.M. and dinner from 6:00 to 8:00 P.M.

The **Caterina de Medici Dining Room** offers fixed-price menus and features contemporary and traditional regional Italian specialties. The restaurant is open Monday through Friday. Lunch is served at 11:30 A.M. and noon. Dinner is served from 6:30 to 7:30 P.M.

The **Escoffier Restaurant** highlights classic French cuisine in an elegant setting and features table-side presentations. It's open Tuesday through Saturday. Lunch is served from noon to 1:00 P.M. and dinner from 6:30 to 8:30 P.M.

The **American Bounty Restaurant** serves a variety of regional American dishes as well as a daily special from the Julia Child Rotisserie kitchen. The restaurant is open Tuesday through Saturday. Lunch is served from 11:30 A.M. to 1:00 P.M. and dinner from 6:30 to 8:30 P.M.

The Culinary Institute of America is at 433 Albany Post Road, Hyde Park 12538, (914) 452-9600. Reservations are recommended at all of the restaurants and can be made by calling (914) 471-6608 Monday through Friday, 8:30 A.M. to 5:00 P.M. Jackets are required at the Escoffier Restaurant. Enter through the main gate and follow signs for the restaurants.

Those who love cooking—or eating—will enjoy poking through **The Culinary Institute of America's Conrad N. Hilton Library,** which opened in September 1993. The $7.5 million, 45,000-square-foot facility houses one of the largest collections of culinary works in the country. In addition to almost 50,000 books, the library has a video viewing center and a video theater. Visitors may see the collections of food writer Craig Claiborne, gastronome George Lang, and acclaimed chef August Guyet.

The Conrad N. Hilton Library is open Monday through Thursday, 8:00 A.M. to 10:00 P.M.; Friday, 8:00 A.M. to 9:00 P.M.; Saturday, 9:00 A.M. to 5:00 P.M.; and Sunday, noon to 8:00 P.M. The research staff is available Monday through Friday from 8:30 A.M. to 5:00 P.M. The library is immediately on your left after you pass through the main gate.

Heading north past Hyde Park, we're back in mansion territory—but with a difference. Homes such as Philipse Manor Hall were built by men whose fortunes were founded in vast landholdings, but palaces such as the ◆ **Mills Mansion** in Staatsburg represent the glory days of industrial and financial captains—the so-called Gilded Age of the late nineteenth century. The idea behind this sort of house building was to live not like a country squire but like a Renaissance doge.

Ogden Mills's neoclassical mansion was finished in 1896, but its story begins more than a hundred years earlier. In 1792 the property on which it stands was

Mills Mansion

purchased by Morgan Lewis, great-grandfather of
Mills's wife, Ruth Livingston Mills. Lewis, an officer in
the revolution and the third postindependence governor of New York State, built two houses here. The first
burned in 1832, at which time it was replaced by an
up-to-date Greek Revival structure. This was the home
that stood on the property when it was inherited by
Ruth Livingston Mills in 1890.

But Ogden Mills had something far grander in mind
for his wife's legacy. He hired a firm with a solid reputation in mansion building to enlarge the home and
embellish its interiors—a popular firm among wealthy

clients, one that went by the name of McKim, Mead, and White.

The architects added two spacious wings and decked out both the new and the old portions of the exterior with balustrades and pilasters more reminiscent of Blenheim Palace than anything previously seen in the Hudson Valley. The interior was (and is) French, in Louis XV and XVI period styles—lots of carving and gilding on furniture and wall and ceiling surfaces, along with oak paneling and monumental tapestries.

The last of the clan to live here was Ogden L. Mills, at one time U.S. secretary of the treasury, who died in 1937. One of his surviving sisters donated the home to the state of New York, which opened it to the public as a state historic site.

The Mills Mansion, off Old Post Road, Staatsburg 12580, (914) 889-8851, is open from mid-April through Labor Day on Wednesday through Saturday, 10:00 A.M. to 5:00 P.M., and on Sunday, noon to 5:00 P.M. From Labor Day through the last Sunday in October, the mansion is open on Wednesday through Sunday, noon to 5:00 P.M. It is also open during the Christmas season. Call for hours. Admission is $3.00 for adults, $2.00 for senior citizens, and $1.00 for children ages 5 to 12.

If touring the area's numerous mansions has left you with "mansionitis," reserve a room at ◆ **Belvedere Mansion,** a grand, hilltop, Greek Revival estate overlooking the Hudson River. Guests can choose one of the beautifully appointed "cottage" rooms—each with its own entrance and private bath—in a separate building facing the mansion, or one of the smaller "cozies. A full country breakfast is served fireside in the winter and, in warmer months, *al fresco* in a pavilion gazebo overlooking a fountain and pond. Bring a bottle of your favorite wine (the restaurant has applied for a liquor license) when dining at the house restaurant, which offers delicacies such as an appetizer of gâteau of wild mushrooms and chèvre with a truffle vinaigrette and entrees such as braised lamb shank with saffron risotto, artichokes, and mint.

Belvedere Mansion in Staatsburg (mailing address: P.O. Box 785, Rhinebeck 12572), (914) 889–8000, is open year-round. Weeknight rates range from $65 for a "cozy" to $125 for the River Queen Cottage (the other cottages rent for $95 weeknights). There is a two-night minimum stay on weekends. Breakfast is included.

◆ **Troutbeck,** on the banks of the trout-filled Webatuck River in Amenia, is an English-style country estate that functions as a corporate conference center during the week and as a country inn on weekends. The 422-acre retreat, with its slate-roofed mansion with leaded windows, is a perfect place for a romantic weekend. There are nine fireplaced bedrooms, many rooms with canopy beds, an oak-paneled library, gardens—even a pool and tennis courts. And, of course, gourmet dining.

The former home of poet-naturalist Myron B. Benton, Troutbeck was a gathering place for celebrities during the early decades of the twentieth century. Ernest Hemingway, Sinclair Lewis, and Teddy

Roosevelt are said to have been houseguests of the Springarn family, who owned the house from 1902 to 1978.

Every weekend, Troutbeck's award-winning chef prepares mouthwatering selections such as escargots with Gorgonzola and apples; grilled sushi tuna mignon over black-olive-and-garlic orzo; or grilled loin of lamb with lentils Dupuy, grilled sweet onions, and port demi-glace; as well as fabulous desserts.

Troutbeck, Leedsville Road, Amenia 12501, (914) 373–9681, is open year-round. Weekend rates, which include two nights lodging, six meals, and open bar, range from $650 to $1,050 a couple.

The Wetmore family, who planted ◆ **Cascade Mountain Vineyards,** say of their product: "Regional wine is a way of tasting our seasons past. Last summer's sunshine, the snows of winter, rain, and frost; it's all there in a glass. . . . " You can sample Hudson Valley's seasons past at the vineyard, which offers tours and tastings daily year-round from 10:00 A.M. to 6:00 P.M. They also serve lunch daily except Wednesday from 11:30 A.M. to 3:00 P.M.; a light menu Sunday through Thursday from 3:00 to 5:00 P.M.; during summer months a happy hour every Friday from 5:00 to 8:00 P.M.; and dinner Saturday from 6:00 to 9:00 P.M.

Don't look for hamburgers on the menu; the kitchen takes pride in serving gourmet meals with a regional touch. Menu samplings include a grilled quail with chive potato salad appetizer and an entree of mustard and rosemary crusted, pan-seared Ahi tuna with herb pesto and sun dried tomato polenta. Happy hour features music, hot and cold hors d'oeuvres, tours and tastings, and, of course, wine.

Cascade Mountain Vineyards is on Flint Hill Road in Amenia 12501, (914) 373-9021.

While its location is off the beaten path, the ◈ **Old Drovers Inn** is very much on the main track for those who love gourmet dining and superb accommodations. Winner of some of the industry's most prestigious awards, including AAA's Four Diamond Award and an award of excellence for its wine list and cellar from *Wine Spectator,* the inn, a Relais and Chateau property, was also named one of the five Gourmet Retreats of the Year in Andrew Harper's *Hideaway Report.*

The beautifully restored colonial inn, in continuous use since it was built in 1750, was originally a stop for cattle drovers, who purchased cattle and swine from New England farmers and drove the animals down the post roads to markets in New York City.

The inn's signature dishes, cheddar cheese soup and browned turkey hash, reflect its colonial heritage. Dinner entrees such as steamed breast of squab and foie gras and medallions of monkfish in langoustine sauce reflect the touch of chef François de Melogue, who is trained in a combination of classical French technique and American regional cuisine.

Like the food, the four guest rooms are elegant. Prices range from $150 midweek for the intimate, antique-filled Rose Room ($320 weekends and holidays) to $230 midweek for the Meeting Room, with a unique barrel-shaped ceiling and fireplace ($395 weekends and holidays). American breakfast is included.

Old Drovers Inn, Dover Plains 12522, (914) 832-9311, serves lunch Friday, Saturday, and Sunday, and dinner nightly, except Wednesday.

When Peter Wing returned from fighting in Vietnam he was twenty-one years old and wanted to build a place where he could retreat from the world. He and his wife, Toni, worked for the next twenty-five years to create ◆ **Wing's Castle,** a fabulously eccentric stone castle overlooking the Hudson Valley. Eighty percent of the structure is made of salvaged materials from antique buildings.

Peter wasn't successful in retreating, however. Visitors from around the world stop in for tours and are surprised to learn that the castle is also the Wings' home. It's furnished with Victorian pieces, more than 2,000 antiques, and mannequins dressed in period clothing. A 7-foot-deep moat that runs under the castle serves as a swimming pool, and 12- and 13-foot handhewn rocks that Peter removed from an old building are arranged in a circle to create Stonehenge East.

Wing's Castle, R.R. 1, Box 174A, Millbrook 12545, (914) 677-9085, is open Wednesday through Sunday May 30 through Christmas, 10:00 A.M. to 5:00 P.M. Tours are given on the half hour. Admission is $5.00 for adults and $3.00 for children ages 4 to 11.

At **Innisfree Garden** eastern design concepts combine with American techniques to create a "cup garden," which has origins in Chinese paintings dating back a thousand years.

The cup garden draws attention to something rare or beautiful, segregating it so that it can be enjoyed without distraction. It can be anything, from a single rock covered with lichens and sedums to a meadow. Each forms a three-dimensional picture. Innisfree Gardens is a series of cup gardens—streams, water-falls, plants—each its own picture and each a visual treat.

Innisfree Garden, Tyrrel Road, Millbrook 12545, (914) 677-8000, is open May 1 to October 20, Wednesday through Friday, 10:00 A.M. to 4:00 P.M. and weekends and legal holidays, 11:00 A.M. to 5:00 P.M. Closed Monday and Tuesday except legal holidays. Admission is $1.00 for those 10 years and over on weekdays and $3.00 on weekends and holidays.

"There I was, minding my own business. I was standing by the side of the road, investigating a potential dinner, when some lunatic in a rusty Plymouth knocked me 10 feet into the air."

Thus begins a column by Elizabeth T. Vulture in the *Raptor Report*, news bulletin of the ◆ **Hudson Valley Raptor Center.** Luckily for Elizabeth—whose vision was never quite the same—she was rescued and given a home at the center. In addition to caring for injured raptors and returning as many as possible to the wild, the center offers the public a chance to meet and learn about all birds of prey, including bald eagles, red-tailed hawks, peregrine falcons, and great horned owls. It houses more than 100 raptors of twenty species, many of whom are threatened or endangered.

The Hudson Valley Raptor Center, South Road, Route 53 (R.R. 1, Box 437B), Stanfordville 12581, (914) 758-6957, is open May through October, Friday through Monday 1:00 to 4:00 P.M. Admission is $7.00 for adults, $5.00 for seniors and students, and $2.50 for children ages 12 and under. Call ahead as hours are subject to change.

The **Old Rhinebeck Aerodrome,** 3 miles upriver from the town of Rhinebeck, is more than just a museum—many of the pre-1930s planes exhibited here actually take to the air each weekend.

The three main buildings at the aerodrome house a collection of aircraft, automobiles, and other vehicles from the period 1900–37 and are open throughout the week. On Saturday and Sunday, though, you can combine a tour of the exhibits on the ground with attendance at an air show featuring both original aircraft and accurate reproductions. Saturdays are reserved for flights of planes from the Pioneer (pre–World War I) and Lindbergh eras. On Sundays the show is a period-piece melodrama in which intrepid Allied fliers do battle with the "Black Baron." Where else can you watch a live dogfight?

All that's left at this point is to go up there yourself, and you can do just that. The aerodrome has on hand a 1929 New Standard D-25—which carries four passengers wearing helmets and goggles—for open-cockpit flights of fifteen minutes' duration. The cost is $30 per person.

Old Rhinebeck Aerodrome, 44 Stone Church Road, Rhinebeck 12572, (914) 758-8610, is open daily, May 15 through the end of October, from 10:00 A.M. to 5:00 P.M. Air shows, from June 15 through October 15, are on Saturdays and Sundays at 2:30 P.M. The fashion show, in which ladies from the audience dress up in vintage clothing, begins at 2:00 P.M. Biplane rides are available before and after the shows. Weekday admission is $4.00 for adults, $2.00 for children ages 6 to 10, and free for children under 6. Admission for weekend air shows is $10 for adults and $5 for children ages 6 to 10. The plane rides cost extra, as mentioned above.

America's oldest continuously operated hotel, the **Beekman Arms,** opened for business as the Traphagen Inn in 1766. A meeting place for American Revolution generals, the Beekman was also the site of Franklin Delano Roosevelt's election eve rallies from the beginning of his career right through his presidency. Visitors can choose from a room in the inn, the motel, or in the **Delamater House** (914-786-7080), built in 1844 and one of the few early examples of American Gothic residences still in existence.

The Beekman Arms, Route 9, Rhinebeck 12572 (914) 876-7077, is open year-round. Rates range from $80 to $140 and all rooms have private bath, TV, phone, and a decanter of sherry.

China Rose, which bills itself as "A Chinese Bistro," actually serves delicious classic dishes from regions throughout China. Among the standouts are Hunan pork dumplings with hot sauce and Peking style duck. For the kids there's lo mein; for those who like it hot, pork in tiger sauce and hot and sour soup. The restaurant, at 100 Schatzel Street, Rhinecliff 12574, (914) 876-7442, opens for dinner nightly at 5:00 P.M. except Tuesday. Reservations aren't accepted so go early.

John and Jan Gilmor create a variety of mouth-blown and hand-pressed stemware, tableware, decorative vessels, and ornaments from glass John formulates from scratch, working with his wife to develop unique colors and finishes. Their pieces are featured in international and presidential collections.

Gilmor Glassworks has showrooms on Route 82, Pine Plains 12567 (518) 398–6678, and at the corner of Routes 22 and 44 in Millerton 12546, (518) 789–6700. Visitors are invited to watch the artists while they work at the glass furnaces at the Millerton location, but are urged to call ahead to find out when the "hot process" can be observed. First quality and irregular pieces are sold in both showrooms. Shop hours are Monday through Friday, 10:00 A.M. to 4:00 P.M.; weekends, 11:00 A.M. to 5:00 P.M.

Crailo Gardens, in the small town of Ancram, near the spot where the borders of New York, Massachusetts, and Connecticut meet, is a place to contemplate earthbound delights rather than aerial excitement. The Crailo Gardens and Nurseries represent more than a quarter-century of devotion on the part of founder Edwin R. Thomson to the cultivation of dwarf and rare conifers. Thomson's collection now exceeds 400 cultivars of *Chamaecyparis, Juniperus, Picea, Pinus, Thuja,* and others; he has some 3,000 plants for sale and starts about 1,000 each year. All of the plants that are available for sale are in containers, with the exception of those in a permanent exhibit area, which is open to the public after 2:00 P.M. on Sunday afternoons. Crailo Gardens is open daylight hours from May through September and during other months, weather permitting. An appointment is advised during off season.

Crailo Gardens is on Route 82, Ancram 12502, (518) 329-0601. Admission is free.

The once-dying town of Tivoli is enjoying a renaissance and has been described by some as "the next Aspen without the hype and pretension." It's home to numerous antiques stores, artists' cooperatives, and excellent restaurants. One, **Cafe Pongo,** serves up some of the best baked goods in the area, as well as homemade soups such as coconut milk gazpacho, delicious sandwiches, signature steam pots like spicy white clam stock over shredded savoy cabbage, and standards such as crab cakes and grilled flank steak. The decor is uniquely elegant but not off-putting for kids; crayons and soap bubbles are provided to keep them happy.

Cafe Pongo, 69 Broadway, Tivoli 12583, (914) 757-4403, is open Tuesday through Friday, 10:00 A.M. to 10:00 P.M.; Saturday and Sunday, 8:00 A.M. to 10:00 P.M.

One of the most exciting recent developments in the professional dance world is the establishment of ◆ **Kaatsban,** a center that—beginning in the spring of 1997—hopes to provide a "permanent, year-round location dedicated to the growth, advancement, and preservation of professional dance." Plans for the 153-acre site overlooking the Hudson River include a 500-seat theater, performance stages, studios, and a dance library.

Kaatsban International Dance Center, P.O. Box 482, Tivoli 12583, will be glad to provide progress reports. Call (914) 657-8392 or 757-5106.

There was a time when every schoolchild worthy of a gold star on his or her reports knew the name *Clermont.* Of course, it was the first successful steamboat, built by Robert Fulton and tested on the Hudson River. Less commonly known, however, is that the boat formally registered by its owners as *The North River Steamboat of Clermont* took its name from the estate of Robert R. Livingston, chancellor of New York and a backer of Fulton's experiments. ◆ **Clermont,** one of the great family seats of the valley, overlooks the Hudson River near Germantown.

The story of Clermont begins with the royal charter granted to Robert Livingston in 1686, which made the Scottish-born trader Lord of the Manor of Livingston, a 162,000-acre tract that would evolve into the entire southern third of modern-day Columbia County. When Livingston died in 1728, he broke with the English custom of strict adherence to primogeniture by giving 13,000 acres of his land to his third son. This was Clermont, the Lower Manor, on which Robert of Clermont, as he was known, established his home in 1728.

Two more Robert Livingstons figure in the tale after this point: Robert of Clermont's son, a New York judge, and *his* son, a member of the Second Continental Congress who filled the now-obsolete office of state chancellor. It was the chancellor's mother, Margaret Beekman Livingston, who rebuilt the house after it was burned in 1777 by the British (parts of the original walls are incorporated into the present structure).

The Livingston family lived at Clermont until

1962, making various enlargements and modifications to their home over time. In that year the house, its furnishings, and the 500 remaining acres of the Clermont estate became the property of the state of New York.

The mansion at Clermont State Historic Site (also a National Historic Landmark) has been restored to its circa 1930 appearance; however, the collections are primarily half eighteenth- and half nineteenth-century French and early American. Tours of Clermont include the first and second floors. An orientation exhibit and a short film are given at the gift shop. There are formal gardens, woodsy hiking trails, and spacious landscapes (perfect for picnics) on bluffs overlooking the Hudson.

Clermont, off Route 9G, Clermont 12526, (518) 537-4240, is open daily except Mondays that are not holidays from April 15 through October, and weekends and the Friday after Thanksgiving from November 1 through April 14. Call ahead for hours of tours. The grounds are open daily year-round from 8:30 A.M. to sunset.

History generally conditions us to expect the great houses of the world to belong to industrialists and landholders, while artists—so the cliché has it—starve in garrets. One artist who built many fanciful garrets and starved in none of them was the Hudson River School master Frederic Edwin Church, whose Persian Gothic castle, ◆ **Olana,** commands a magnificent view of the river south of the town of Hudson. What the popular landscape painter did here was nothing less than sculpt the perfect embodiment of his tastes and then go on to live in it for the rest of his life.

Olana draws heavily upon Islamic and Byzantine motifs. Persian arches abound, as do Oriental carpets, brasswork, and inlaid furniture. The overall setting is typically Victorian, with no space left empty that could possibly be filled with things. What makes Olana untypical, of course, is the quality of the things.

Although Church employed as a consultant Calvert Vaux, who had collaborated with Frederick Law Olmsted on the design of New York's Central Park, the artist was the architect of his own house. When scholars describe Olana as a major work of art by Church, they are not speaking figuratively; the paints for the interior were mixed on his own palette.

Olana

Olana, Route 9G, Hudson 12534, (518) 828–0135, is open *by guided tour only* from April 15 to Labor Day, Wednesday through Sunday. The first tour begins at 10:00 A.M. weekdays and Saturday and noon on Sunday; the last tour starts at 4:00 P.M. Also open on Memorial Day, Independence Day, and Labor Day. Call for September and October hours. Tours are limited to twelve people, so call for reservations. An admission fee is charged. The grounds are open year-round from 8:00 A.M. until sunset.

EAST OF ALBANY

The ✦**Shaker Museum and Library,** in Old Chatham, is housed in a collection of buildings located just 12 miles from Mt. Lebanon, New York, where the Shakers established their first community.

The Shakers, formally known as the United Society of Believers in Christ's Second Appearing, were a sect founded in Britain and transplanted to America just prior to the revolution. A quietist, monastic order dedicated to equality between the sexes, sharing of community property, temperance in its broad sense, and the practice of celibacy, the sect peaked in the middle nineteenth century with about 6,000 members. Today there are fewer than a dozen Shakers living in a community at Sabbathday Lake, Maine.

Ironically, it is the secular aspects of Shaker life that are most often recalled today. The members of the communities were almost obsessive regarding simplicity and purity of form in the articles they designed and crafted for daily life; "Shaker furniture" has become a generic term for the elegantly uncluttered designs they employed. In their pursuit of the perfect form dictated by function, they even invented now-ubiquitous objects such as the flat broom.

The Shaker Museum has amassed a collection of more than 18,000 objects, half of which are on display. The main building contains an orientation gallery that surveys Shaker history and provides highlights of the rest of the collection. The museum's library contains one of the two most extensive collections of Shaker material in the world. The cafe serves snacks and beverages.

The Shaker Museum and Library, Shaker Museum Road (off County Route 13), Old Chatham 12136, (518) 794-9100, is open daily except Tuesday May 1 through October 31, from 10:00 A.M. to 5:00 P.M. Admission is $6.00 for adults, $5.00 for senior citizens, $3.00 for children ages 8 to 17, and free for children under 8. Family admission is $14.00.

In 1624 Dutchmen sailed up the Hudson River and established a fur trading station called Fort Orange at present-day Albany. Within twenty-five years it was a thriving community. Across the river is the town of Rensselaer, named for the family who held the "patroonship," or feudal proprietorship, of the vast area on the east bank. ◆ **Crailo,** built in the early eighteenth century by the Patroon's grandson, recalls a time when the Dutch were still the predominant cultural presence in the area.

Crailo changed with time and tastes. A Georgian-style east wing added in 1762 reflected the increasing influence of the English in the area. Federal touches were added later in the century. Since 1933 the house has served as a museum of the Dutch in the upper Hudson Valley. Exhibits include seventeenth- and eighteenth-century prints and archaeological artifacts, many from the Fort Orange excavation of 1970–1971.

Crailo, 9½ Riverside Avenue, Rensselaer 12144, (518) 463-8738, is open mid-April through late October, Wednesday through Saturday from 10:00 A.M. to 5:00 P.M. and Sunday from 1:00 to 5:00 P.M. Tours are given on the hour and half-hour; the last tour is at 4:00 P.M. It is also open Memorial Day, Independence Day, and Labor Day. Call for off-season hours and other information. Admission is $3.00 for adults, $1.00 for children ages 5 to 12, and $2.00 per person for tour buses.

Natural and social history are the focus of a Troy institution geared specifically to young people. This is ❖ **The Junior Museum,** a hands-on learning center that has everything from a reproduction of a circa 1850 log cabin to constellation shows in the planetarium.

The main gallery of the museum features annually changing art, history, and science exhibits. Upstairs, in addition to the cabin, is a gallery of physical and natural science exhibits that include honeybees in an observation hive, a red-tailed hawk, live reptiles, and both salt- and freshwater aquariums. Downstairs the major exhibit is entitled "Balanced on the Back of a Turtle," with a longhouse, Iroquois stories, hunting, harvesting, and lots of hands-on fun.

The Junior Museum, 282 Fifth Avenue, Troy 12182, (518) 235-2120, is open Wednesday through Sunday, noon until 5:00 P.M. Admission is $3.00. Children under 2 are free. It includes shows in the planetarium and shows with live animals.

HOOSIC VALLEY

Most of us know that the Battle of Bunker Hill was not actually fought on Bunker Hill (it took place on Breed's Hill, also in Charlestown, Massachusetts), but how many can identify another military misnomer of the revolution?

We're talking about the 1777 Battle of Bennington, an American victory that laid the groundwork for the defeat and surrender of General Burgoyne at Saratoga that October. The battle, in which American militia-men defended their ammunition and supplies from an attacking party made up of British troops, Tory sympathizers, mercenaries, and Indians, took place not in Bennington, Vermont, but in Walloomsac, New York. True, the stores that the British were after were stashed in the Vermont town, but the actual fighting took place on New York soil.

The state of New York today maintains the site of the battle as an official state historic site. It's on a lovely hilltop in eastern Rensselaer County, studded with bronze and granite markers that explain the movements of the troops on the American militia's triumphal day. The spot is located on the north side of Route 67 and is open throughout the year during daylight hours, weather permitting. Visitors can check road conditions by calling **Bennington Battlefield** at (518) 686-7109. On a clear day one can enjoy fine views of the Green Mountain foothills, prominent among which is Bennington's obelisk monument. Drive over to visit the monument and give the Vermonters their due—but really, doesn't "Battle of Walloomsac" have a nice ring to it?

Will Moses, a direct descendant of the renowned primitive painter Grandma Moses, is a folk artist whose minutely detailed paintings reflect the charm and beauty of the tiny rural community where he lives. Lithographs, printed by master lithographers from original oil paintings done by Will, are exhibited and sold, along with offset prints, at ❖ **Mt. Nebo Gallery,** Grandma Moses Road, Eagle Bridge 12057, (518) 686-4334. The gallery is open Monday through Friday, 9:00 A.M. to 4:00 P.M.; Saturday, 10:00 A.M. to 5:00 P.M.; and Sunday, noon to 5:00 P.M.

Our next stop on this ramble up the east shore of the Hudson offers proof that in this part of the world, the monastic spirit did not pass into history with the Shakers. Cambridge is the home of the ❖ **New Skete Communities,** a group of monks, nuns, and laypeople organized around a life of prayer, contemplation, and physical work. Founded in 1966 within the Byzantine Rite of the Roman Catholic church, the New Skete Communities have been a part of the Orthodox church in America since 1979.

Visitors to New Skete are welcome at the community's two houses of worship. The small Temple of the Transfiguration of Christ, open at all times, contains a number of icons painted by the monks and nuns, while the larger Church of Christ the Wisdom of God—open to visitors only during services—has, imbedded in its marble floor, original pieces of mosaic that were brought from the A.D. 576 Church of Sancta Sophia (Holy Wisdom) in Constantinople. Worship services are usually twice daily.

As with many monastic communities, the monks and the nuns of New Skete help support themselves through a wide variety of pursuits. An important part of their life is the breeding of German shepherds and the boarding and training of all breeds. The monks have even written two successful books, *How to Be Your Dog's Best Friend* and *The Art of Raising a Puppy*. At their gift shop, they sell their own cheeses, smoked meats, fruitcake, the famous New Skete cheesecakes made by the nuns, and original painted icons.

The New Skete Communities are in Cambridge 12816. The nuns are accessible from the village of Cambridge via East Main Street on Ash Grove Road, and the monks farther along to Chestnut Woods Road and then New Skete Road. For information call the monks at (518) 677-3928 or the nuns at (518) 677-3810

At the ◆ **Log Village Grist Mill,** built in 1810 by Hezekiah Mann, a 17-foot wooden waterwheel still provides power to three millstones that grind cornmeal, wheat flour, and buckwheat. A museum in the mill barn houses an exhibit of old farm machinery and household items, and the cider mill, built in 1894, still has the original cider press—powered by a 7 horsepower single-cylinder gas engine. Have a picnic, take a tour, and watch as many "obsolete" machines crank and grind their way toward the twenty-first century.

The Log Village Grist Mill, County Route 30, East Hartford 12838, (518) 632-5237, is open weekdays Memorial Day weekend through October 15, and weekdays by appointment.

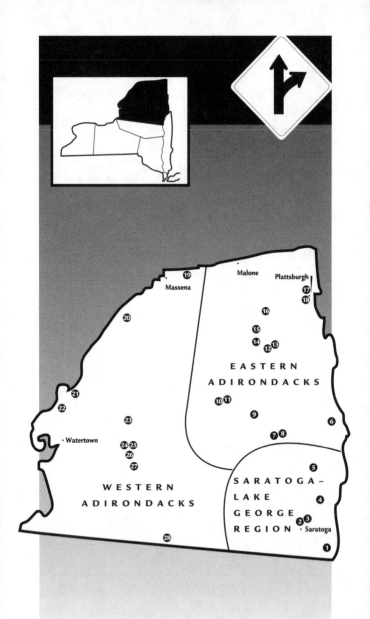

THE ADIRONDACKS

1. Saratoga National Historical Park
2. National Museum of Racing and Thoroughbred Hall of Fame
3. Petrified Sea Gardens
4. Hyde Collection
5. Marcella Sembrich Opera Museum
6. Fort Ticonderoga
7. Garnet Hill Lodge
8. Highwinds Inn
9. Adirondack Museum
10. Bird's Boat Livery
11. Sagamore
12. Mt. Van Hoevenburg Olympic Sports Complex
13. John Brown Farm State Historic Site
14. Hathaway Boat Shop
15. Somewhere Farms
16. Six Nations Indian Museum
17. Kent-Delord House
18. Yarborough Square
19. Akwesasne Cultural Center
20. Frederic Remington Art Museum
21. Boldt Castle
22. Antique Boat Museum
23. American Maple Museum
24. North American Fiddler's Hall of Fame & Museum
25. Whetstone Gulf State Park
26. Greystone Manor
27. Constable Hall
28. Steuben Memorial State Historic Site

THE ADIRONDACKS

North of the Mohawk Valley, spread between Lake Champlain and the St. Lawrence River, New York's Adirondack Mountains comprise one of the nation's great expanses of near-wilderness and surely the largest slice of backcountry in the northeastern states. The state-protected Adirondack Forest Preserve alone accounts for more than 2 million acres of mountains, woodlands, and lakes, and this is only part of the 6-million-acre Adirondack State Park. For sheer vastness and emptiness, the Adirondack region is rivaled in this part of the country only by the northern interior of Maine; but while inland Maine—except for Mount Katahdin—is generally flat or gently rolling, the northern counties of New York contain forty-two peaks more than 4,000 feet in height. (The highest is Mt. Marcy, near Lake Placid, at 5,344 feet.) As in northern Maine, parts of the Adirondacks are still logged, although many areas have returned to a near-approximation of what they looked like when white men first saw them.

Ironically, the Adirondacks have benefited from being left on the sidelines during the "discovery" of nearby Vermont and New Hampshire in the years following World War II. The two New England states have acquired a certain cachet, and they have been more heavily developed and populated as a result. The equally beautiful Adirondacks, meanwhile, have drifted along in the public consciousness largely as the place where the famous summer chairs come from (it seems they really did originate here) and as the locale for Gilded Age "camps" on estates running into the tens of thousands of acres. Throw in the Thousand Islands, Saranac Lake, and Lakes Placid and George, and the perception is complete.

But there's so much more. In addition to being a "hidden" wilderness recreation land of such vast proportions, the Adirondacks played their part in history as well, from the French and Indian Wars through the American Revolution and the War of 1812. Once a point of friction between British Canada and the United States, today's border is marked by the engineering marvel of the St. Lawrence Seaway and by the binational resort area that has sprung up around the Thousand Islands. The south-eastern gateway to the Adirondacks, Saratoga, is one of the horse-racing capitals of America. Farther north are museums that chronicle the life of the Iroquois, the art of Frederic Remington, and Adirondacks craftsmanship, boatbuilding, and pioneer life.

Head north beyond Saratoga, then, for the real "upstate" New York, a domain that rivals the expansiveness of the West yet is rooted in the traditions of the East.

(*Note:* The overall place-to-place direction followed in this chapter is counterclockwise—south to north to west.)

SARATOGA–
LAKE GEORGE REGION

North of the confluence of the Mohawk and Hudson rivers, near the present-day towns of Mechanicville and Stillwater, one of the most decisive battles of world history was fought in the early days of October 1777. The Battle of Saratoga holds its place in history as a watershed, a turning point in the prolonged and peripatetic series of military campaigns that made up the American Revolution. The battle, the sites of which are commemorated in ◆ **Saratoga National Historical Park,** offered the first conclusive proof that American forces could triumph over the British in a major engagement and led to the French entering the war on behalf of the United States.

The Lake Champlain and Hudson River valleys were a major north-south route in the eighteenth century and consequently provided a natural highway for the movement of troops. British General John Burgoyne planned, early in 1777, to move his forces southward from Canada to Albany, from which point he would be able to act in concert with the British army headquartered in New York to cut the New England colonies off from the Middle Atlantic region.

But Burgoyne's plan ran into trouble from the start. He was denied the support of a detachment under Colonel Barry St. Leger proceeding east from Lake Ontario, after St. Leger retreated back to Canada in the face of an expected attack by General Benedict Arnold (Arnold was not yet the traitor of historical record). Burgoyne also suffered a surprise defeat when he sent part of his army into the field against New England militia at the Battle of Bennington, August 16. By the time he reached the west bank of the Hudson at Saratoga (present-day Schuylerville) on September 13, the prospect of "Gentleman Johnny" Burgoyne making an easy progress to Albany was considerably dimmed by the presence of 9,000 American troops, with artillery, guarding the Hudson River route at Bemis Heights.

Burgoyne was stopped in a standoff battle on September 19. He regrouped his forces a mile north of the American lines for a three-week period of waiting for reinforcements from New York. But help didn't arrive, and rather than allow his supplies to become even more depleted and his men more demoralized, Burgoyne again engaged the Americans in battle on October 7. The fighting ended with a thousand British casualties (the Americans suffered fewer than half that number) and a Redcoat retreat north to the Saratoga heights. It was there that Burgoyne, his 6,000 troops surrounded by 20,000 Americans, surrendered on October 17.

A 10-mile tour road in the 3,200-acre Saratoga National Historical Park encompasses the sites that were crucial during those fateful weeks in September and October 1777. The 1777 Philip Schuyler House and the Neilson House can be toured in summer months.

Saratoga National Historical Park Visitor Center, 648 Route 32, Stillwater 12170, (518) 664-9821, is open daily year-round from 9:00 A.M. to 5:00 P.M. Between May and October 31, admission is $4.00 per car for the tour road; $2.00 for hiking. The tour road is open from early April through late November. Children 16 and under are admitted free.

Tradition says the Indians of the Saratoga region visited High Rock Spring as early as 1300 to gain strength from the "Medicine Spring of the Great

Spirit." Four hundred and seventy years later, in 1771, Sir William Johnson, suffering from a wound received in the Battle of Lake George, was carried on a litter by Mohawk Indians from Johnstown to High Rock Spring. After a short stay his health improved noticeably, and the reputation of the spring quickly grew.

The first person to recognize the commercial value of the mineral waters at Saratoga Springs may well have been John Arnold, who in 1774 purchased a crude log cabin built on a bluff overlooking High Rock Spring, improved it, and opened an inn. Thirteen years later, in 1787, revolutionary war hero Alexander Bryan purchased the inn. He is generally recognized as the first permanent white resident of Saratoga Springs, and his inn was the only Saratoga hotel until 1801, when Gideon Putnam built the Grand Union Hotel. Throughout the years the inn has operated sporadically as a lodge, tavern, restaurant, and private dwelling. Today you can enjoy prime rib, fettuccini Lily, or a host of other delicious dishes at **The Olde Bryan Inn.**

The Olde Bryan Inn, 123 Maple Avenue, Saratoga Springs 12866, (518) 587-2990, is open Monday through Friday from 11:00 A.M. until 11:00 P.M.; Friday and Saturday until midnight. The tavern is open daily until 1:00 A.M.

Between 1823 and 1889 mineral waters from approximately thirty springs in Saratoga County were bottled and distributed around the world, and an industry was born. The **National Bottle Museum,** housed in a 1901 former hardware store in Ballston Spa's historic district, documents the rise and decline

The Olde Bryan Inn

of that industry. Through exhibits of antique bottles and glassmaking tools, videos, and artifacts, it tells the story of a time past, when young men were indentured to the owners of glass factories and apprenticed for fifteen years in order to become glassblowers in the glasshouses that made bottles and jars by hand. It recreates an industry and a way of life that have vanished from the American scene.

The National Bottle Museum, 76 Milton Avenue, Ballston Spa 12020, (518) 885-7589, is open daily from June 1 to September 30, 10:00 A.M. to 4:00 P.M.; October 1 to May 31, open Monday through Friday,

10:00 A.M. to 4:00 P.M., and closed weekends. Admission is $2.00 for adults, $1.00 for children ages 6 to 12, and free for children under 6.

After a nice mineral bath and massage at Saratoga Spa State Park, you'll be all set for a night at the track. Horse racing is Saratoga's other raison d'être, and the history and traditions of the sport are thoroughly chronicled at the ◆ **National Museum of Racing and Thoroughbred Hall of Fame,** directly across from the Saratoga Race Course. Patrons enter the museum through an actual starting gate, complete with life-size representations of a horse, jockey, and starter. Some of the highlights: paintings of outstanding horses, the saddle and boots used by jockey Johnny Loftus on Man o' War, a Hall of Fame, and the actual skeleton of a thoroughbred. *Race America*, filmed at racetracks and stud farms across the country, is shown in the theater. Video booths lining the walls provide films of some of racing's greats.

The National Museum of Racing and Thoroughbred Hall of Fame, Union Avenue, Saratoga Springs 12866, (518) 584-0400, is open year-round. From January 1 through the end of July, open Monday through Saturday, 10:00 A.M. to 4:30 P.M., and Sunday, noon to 4:30 P.M.; racing season, open daily, 9:00 A.M. to 5:00 P.M.; and September 1 through December 31, open Monday through Saturday, 10:00 A.M. to 4:30 P.M., and Sunday, noon to 4:30 P.M. Admission is $2.00 for adults and $1.00 for senior citizens, students, and children 5 to 18.

The ◆ **Petrified Sea Gardens** consists of the exposed remains of a sea reef that thrived here beneath the Cambrian Sea 500 million years ago, give or take a year or two. Known since 1825 and properly identified in 1883, the "gardens" are the fossilized remains of cabbagelike plants related to modern algae. The reef they formed when alive teemed with trilobites, brachiopods, and rudimentary snails, the fossils of some of which are visible among the plant fossils at this site. When the primordial seas receded, the vegetation was exposed, fossilized beneath layers of sediment, and eventually exposed again by the shearing action of the glaciers.

At the Petrified Sea Gardens visitors can walk among these ancient plants, which can easily be distinguished by the untrained eye. Just look for gray, layered nodules that look as if they might be broken, protruding sections of petrified cabbage. Among the vegetation is the "Iroquois Pine," one of the largest in the Adirondacks and estimated to be 300 years old. There are hands-on activities for children in the nature center.

Petrified Sea Gardens, Petrified Sea Gardens Road, off Route 29, Saratoga Springs 12866, (518) 584-7102, is open Mother's Day to November, daily, 10:00 A.M. to 5:00 P.M. Admission is $2.50 for adults, $2.00 for senior citizens, and $1.25 for children 6 to 16. Call for group rates.

In June 1885, suffering from throat cancer and longing for fresh air and a healthier climate, President Ulysses S. Grant left his home in New York City for Saratoga County. He and his family moved into a summer cottage on top of Mt. McGregor, 8 miles from Saratoga Springs. At the cottage he continued work on his memoirs and, two weeks after completing them, died on July 23, 1885.

The house at **Grant Cottage State Historic Site** is preserved as Grant left it, from the bed where he died to the floral pieces sent from around the country. It is operated by The Friends of the Ulysses S. Grant Cottage, in cooperation with the New York State Office of Parks, Recreation, and Historic Preservation.

Grant Cottage State Historic Site, Mt. McGregor, Wilton (mailing address: P.O. Box 990, Saratoga Springs 12866), (518) 587–8277, is open from Memorial Day to Labor Day, Wednesday through Sunday, 10:00 A.M. to 4:00 P.M.; September, open weekends, 10:00 A.M. to 4:00 P.M. Groups, by advance reservation, are accepted year-round. Admission is $2.00 for adults, $1.50 for senior citizens, and $1.00 for children.

Just north of Saratoga, where so much turn-of-the-century money was spent on the sporting life, is the town of Glens Falls, where a small fortune was instead disbursed on a remarkable collection of art. Glens Falls was the home of Charlotte Pruyn, heiress to a local paper fortune, who married Louis Fiske Hyde of Boston in 1901. In 1907 the Hydes returned to Glens Falls, and in 1912 they began building the Florentine villa that today houses the ◆**Hyde Collection.** Influenced by the home-as-museum philosophy of the Boston tastemaker Isabella Stewart Gardner, and with the help of connoisseurs such as Bernard Berenson, the Hydes filled their home with an eclectic and assiduously acquired collection of American and European art spanning five centuries.

The Hydes bought art with experts' eyes, concentrating not so much upon any individual period or school but upon the most expressive work of whichever painter or sculptor caught their attention. The end result was a collection that appears to have been amassed not by members of the upstate gentry but by a prince with a state treasury at his disposal.

The Hyde Collection opened its doors to the public after Mrs. Hyde's death, at the age of ninety-six, in 1963.

And so it is that in Glens Falls you can enjoy works by artists such as Rubens, Botticelli, Rembrandt, Seurat, Degas, Homer, Whistler, Picasso, Cézanne, and Matisse.

The Hyde Collection, 161 Warren Street, Glens Falls 12801, (518) 792-1761, is open Tuesday through Sunday, 10:00 A.M. to 5:00 P.M.; closed Monday and national holidays. Admission is free.

To really get an off-the-beaten-path view of the Adirondacks, get a horse. **Bennett's Riding Stable** conducts guided trail rides—everything from a one-hour ride for $17, to a 2½-hour ride up Beech Mountain for $35, to a full-day ride for $100. Reservations are advised and families are welcome (helmets are provided). The stable is on Route 9N in Lake Luzerne 12846, (518) 696-4444.

At the age of nineteen, Marcella (Kochanska) Sembrich made her operatic debut in Athens, singing in a number of the great opera houses in Europe before joining New York's Metropolitan Opera Company for its first season in 1883. She returned to Europe until 1898 and then rejoined the Metropolitan Opera until 1909, when her farewell was the occasion for the most sumptuous gala in the Met's history. She was founder of the vocal departments of the Juilliard School in New York and the Curtis Institute in Philadelphia and was a preeminent teacher of singing for twenty-five years. She often brought students to a studio near her summer home in Bolton Landing on Lake George. The ◆ **Marcella Sembrich Opera Museum,** in Mme. Sembrich's converted studio, displays operatic memorabilia she collected from her debut to her death in 1935.

Summer events include studio talks, a lakeside lecture series, a master class in voice, and occasional recitals or chamber concerts.

The Marcella Sembrich Opera Museum, Route 9N, Bolton Landing 12814, (518) 644-9839 (office: P.O. Box 417, Bolton Landing, NY 12814, 518-644-2492), is open daily June 15 through September 15, 10:00 A.M. to 12:30 P.M. and 2:00 to 5:30 P.M. Admission is $2.00.

EASTERN ADIRONDACKS

◆ **Fort Ticonderoga,** which stands on a promontory jutting into the southern end of Lake Champlain, was built by the French in 1755 when the colonial administration in Quebec needed a southern defense in its struggle against Great Britain for control of Canada. Called Fort Carillon, it was built of earth and timbers in the classic French fortress design, and later upgraded to stone, with four pointed bastions presenting an interlocking field of fire against attackers.

In 1758 the Marquis de Montcalm repelled a massive attack by the British, but a year later Lord Jeffery Amherst captured the fort and renamed it "Ticonderoga." Seventeen years later—three weeks after the battles of Lexington and Concord—Ethan Allen and Benedict Arnold captured "Fort Ti" from the British "in the name of the Great Jehovah and the Continental Congress," giving the Americans their first victory of the revolution.

Last garrisoned in 1777, Fort Ti might be little more than a roadside marker had it not been for the efforts of the Pell family to protect the site since 1820 and the commitment of Stephen and Sarah Pell to restore it beginning in 1908. At today's handsome reconstruction, guides in eighteenth-century clothing and a host of events, such as live artillery demonstrations and Fife and Drum musters, help bring the fort to life.

Visitors can stride along the ramparts, view the earthworks built during both the French and Indian War and the American Revolution, examine the barracks, and visit the museum, which houses North America's largest collection of eighteenth-century artillery as well as paintings, furniture, and military memorabilia. Just outside the fort is the battlefield where, in 1758, Montcalm devastated the 42nd Highland ("Black Watch") regiment.

Tours of the 600-acre garrison grounds, offered daily, include the "King's Garden," one of the oldest gardens in the country. Throughout the season there are numerous special events, including a Grand Encampment of the French and Indian War in late June, a Memorial Military Tatoo the weekend following the Fourth of July, and a Revolutionary War Encampment in September. Call for information.

As a sidelight to a Fort Ticonderoga visit, drive to the summit of nearby **Mt. Defiance** for a panoramic view of the Champlain Valley. Hop aboard the M/V *Carillon* to visit **Mount Independence,** a Revolutionary War fort, across Lake Champlain in Vermont.

Fort Ticonderoga, Route 74, Ticonderoga 12883, (518) 585–2821, is open from May through October. May, June, September, and October hours are 9:00 A.M. to 5:00 P.M.; July and August hours are 9:00 A.M. to 6:00 P.M. Admission is $8.00 for adults, $6.00 for children ages 7 to 13, and free for children under 7.

Located west of Ticonderoga, deeper in the Adirondacks, ◆ **Garnet Hill Lodge** is a remote resort on 600 acres of land. The architecture of the main lodge is rustic Adirondack-style, but some of the rooms, complete with whirlpool baths and hot tubs, are anything but rustic. The resort offers a host of activities, including tubing, mountain biking, and a special course on fly-fishing. The lodge, at 13th Lake Road in North River 12856, (800) 497–4207, is open year-round.

The lodge was built by members of the Barton family in 1933 when they came to the area to mine garnet. Today visitors can tour the **Barton Mines** and look for gemstones in the open pits. Call the mines at (518) 251–2706 for information.

Really want to get away from it all? Rent one of the two "little cabins in the woods" without running water or electricity at ◆ **Highwinds Inn,** located on more than 1,600 acres of wilderness on the back of Gore Mountain. The cabins, which accommodate up to six people, rent for $60 a night. The inn also has four modern rooms in the inn and serves dinner to the public nightly (bring your own wine), with specialties such as sautéed calamari with a lemon, scallion, and tomato sauce, and baked herb polenta. The inn is on Barton Mines Road in North River 12856, (518) 251–3760 and advance reservations for both accommodations and meals are a must.

At **Jasco Minerals** Jim and Judy Shaw sell minerals and fossils from around the world, and Judy, a gemologist, handcrafts jewelry. The shop, on Route 28 in North River 12856, (518) 251–3196, is open year-round, weather permitting: July and August from 9:00 A.M. to 7:00 P.M. and the rest of the year from 9:00 A.M. to 5:00 P.M. If the shop isn't open, knock on the door or yell.

Brandied French toast with sautéed apples is the breakfast specialty at **Goose Pond Inn,** a charming, antique-filled, turn-of-the-century B & B just a mile from Gore Mountain Ski Center. The inn, open year-round, is on Main Street in North Creek 12853, (518) 251–3434.

The folks restoring **North Creek Railroad Station** aren't sure when their work will be done, but they've completed much of the exterior work on the station where Vice President Theodore Roosevelt began his journey back to Washington, D.C., after President McKinley was shot. The "stick style" station, built in 1874, was the northernmost terminus of the Adirondack Railroad.

For some distance north of Ticonderoga, Lake Champlain remains narrow enough for a single military installation to have commanded both shores and governed the passage of ship traffic in the eighteenth century. This was the purpose of the fortifications that now lie in ruins at **Crown Point State Historic Site.**

In the late 1600s the staging area for French raids on English settlements in New England and the Hudson Valley, Crown Point became the location of the French Fort St. Frederic, begun in 1734 and finished in 1737. The fort was designed as a stone citadel within outer walls, defended by 50 cannons and swivel-mounted guns and a garrison of 80 to 120 soldiers.

In 1759 General Jeffrey Amherst seized the fort for the British, after it was abandoned by the French, and ordered it enlarged. In 1775 American militiamen captured the fort from the British and used it as headquarters for the Navy under Benedict Arnold until 1776.

The survival of the walls, foundations, and partial structures that we see at Crown Point today is due to the 1910 conveyance of the property to the state by private owners who wished to see the ruins preserved. In 1975 the area officially became a state historic site. The following year the new visitor center and museum were opened. Highlights of the museum exhibits include artifacts uncovered at the site during extensive archaeological digs.

Crown Point State Historic Site, at the Lake Champlain Bridge, 4 miles east of Routes 9N and 22, Crown Point 12928, (518) 597–3666, is open May through October, Wednesday through Saturday, 10:00 A.M. to 5:00 P.M.; Sunday, 1:00 to 5:00 P.M. Also open Memorial Day, Independence Day, and Labor Day. Open during the rest of the year by appointment only. Grounds are accessible all year. There is a $4.00 admission fee for each car. Group visits by advance reservation.

Most museums seek to interpret a particular era, if history is their subject, or the artifacts surround-

ing a particular event or series of events. Not so the
◆ **Adirondack Museum** at Blue Mountain Lake in
the heart of the mountain region. This institution's
ambition, at which it has succeeded admirably, is the
chronicling of the entire Adirondacks experience
throughout the years in which the area has been
known to humanity. Located on a peninsula jutting
into Blue Mountain Lake, the museum rambles
through twenty-two separate exhibit buildings on a
30-acre compound and has been called the finest
regional museum in the United States.

The museum takes as its focus the ways in which
people have related to this incomparable setting and
made their lives here over the past two centuries. As
befits an institution that began in an old hotel, the
museum tells the story of how the Adirondacks were
discovered by vacationists in the nineteenth century,
especially after the 1892 completion of the first railroad through the region.

Examples of nineteenth-century hotel and cabin
rooms are shown, and a restored turn-of-the-century
cottage houses a large collection of rustic "Adirondack
Furniture," currently enjoying a revival among interior
designers. Financier August Belmont's private railroad
car *Oriental*—a reminder of the days when grand conveyances brought the very wealthy to even grander
Adirondack mansions and clubs—is also on exhibit.

The workaday world of the Adirondacks is also
recalled in mining, logging, and boatbuilding exhibits.
The museum possesses an excellent collection of
handmade canoes and guideboats, including some of
the lightweight masterpieces of nineteenth-century

canoe-builder J. H. Rushton. The lovely sloop *Water Witch* is preserved under its own glass dome.

Special attention is given to what has been written and painted using Adirondacks subjects. The museum's picture galleries display the work of artists from the Hudson River School and later periods.

The Adirondack Museum, Route 28N/30, Blue Mountain Lake 12812, (518) 352–7311, is open daily from Memorial Day through mid-October, 9:30 A.M. to 5:30 P.M. Admission is charged.

Studying a subject in a museum is a great way to learn about it. But experience is often the best teacher—even the best museum in the world can't convey how it *feels* to walk among mountains that are 1.3 billion years old. **Siamese Ponds Wilderness Region** in western Warren County is a wilderness area in the true sense of the word: There are hundreds of miles of state-maintained trails and tote roads winding over hills and mountains, past streams, ponds, and lakes. Rockhounds will love exploring the passageways and valleys through a wide variety of rock formations. They were carved by glaciers of the Ice Age and by erosion caused by aeons of tumbling rocks carried along mountain streams, and hikers have found numerous exposed veins of minerals and semiprecious stones.

Siamese Ponds Wilderness Region has entrance points from Stony Creek, Thurman, Wevertown, Johnsburg, North Creek, and North River. Information is available in the *Guide to Adirondack Trails: Central Region,* published by the Adirondack Mountain Club, RD 3, Box 3055, Luzerne Road, Lake George 12845;

(518) 668–4447. Or contact the Gore Mountain Region Chamber of Commerce, P.O. Box 84, North Creek 12853; (518) 251–2612.

Much of the 98-mile-long shoreline of Raquette Lake is inaccessible by road. But everyone knows the U.S. Mail always gets through—this time with the help of the Bird family, who has been providing mail service since 1942. The original delivery boat was a Gar Wood speedboat. Today, grandchildren Joe and Mark Bird deliver the mail Monday through Saturday in the fifty-passenger covered pontoon boat, *Sea Bird*. As they make deliveries to the camps that dot the mostly unde-veloped shoreline, Joe, a fifth-generation Raquette Laker, peppers his narrative of the lake's history with personal anecdotes of local legend and lore.

◆ **Bird's Boat Livery** is on Route 28, Raquette Lake 13436, (315) 354–4441. The mail boat leaves Monday through Saturday in July and August at 10:15 A.M. and stays out for 2 to 2½ hours. The fare is $8.00 for adults and $4.00 for children under 12. Passengers are invited to bring along a picnic lunch. The Birds are happy to give tours by reservation at other times of the year. The livery also rents canoes, pontoons, motor and pedal boats, Fun Jets, and sells bait.

◆ **Sagamore,** on Raquette Lake, is a "prototypical" Adirondack Great Camp. The National Historic Site with twenty-seven buildings was built in 1897 by William West Durant, who sold it in 1901 to Alfred Vanderbilt as a wilderness retreat. After Vanderbilt died on the *Lusitania* in 1915, his widow continued to entertain family and friends as "the hostess of the gaming crowd" for the next thirty-nine years.

Visitors to Sagamore can take a two-hour guided tour and, with reservations, stay overnight in one of the double occupancy rooms (twin beds, bathroom down the hall). Buffet meals are served in the dining hall overlooking the lake. There are 20 miles of hiking trails, canoeing, and a semi-outdoor bowling alley! Request a program catalog to learn about special events.

Sagamore, P.O. Box 146, Raquette Lake 13436, (315) 354-4303, has guided tours at 10:00 A.M. and 1:30 P.M. daily from July Fourth to Labor Day and weekends from Labor Day to Columbus Day. There is a fee. Should you wish to stay overnight, the proprietors remind you that "Sagamore is not a hotel, motel, or resort. It is, instead, a complete experience in living a 'bit of history' in an incomparable setting."

The Artworks, an artists' cooperative on Main Street in downtown Old Forge, features art and craftwork by Adirondack artists. Media include pottery, stained glass, jewelry, fine arts, basketry, folk art, fabric art, and photography. The shop is open daily, year-round. For information call (315) 369-2007.

"A Living Museum of Functional and Aesthetic Necessities: Everything from Abacuses to Zoom Binoculars" is how **Old Forge Hardware** describes itself. "The Adirondacks' Most General Store," serving the area since 1900, is fun to poke through anytime, but it's a haven on a rainy day. Old Forge Hardware, Main Street, Old Forge 13420, (315) 369-6100, is open daily year-round except Christmas Day, New Year's Day, Thanksgiving Day, and Easter.

If hurtling down a track on a tiny sled at speeds in excess of 45 miles per hour is your idea of fun, visit the

◆ **Mt. Van Hoevenburg Olympic Sports Complex.**
From mid-December through mid-March you can
choose from five rides, including: a ½- or 1-mile bobsled run, the one-person luge rocket or four-person ice
rocket, or—the ultimate thrill—a 1-mile, one-minute
bobsled ride that reaches speeds of more than 80 miles
per hour. (This one is by advance reservation only!)
Visiting in the summer? On Summer Storm you plum-
met down the half-mile track aboard a rubber-wheeled
bobsled.

Drive up Whiteface Veterans Memorial Highway to
the summit of the state's fifth highest peak, and either
hike up the stone stairway to the observation tower at
the summit or hop aboard an elevator that climbs 276
feet up through the granite heart of the mountain to
the top.

In town, visit the 1932–1980 **Lake Placid Winter
Olympic Museum** and/or take a tour of all of the
other sites. If you want to see it all, consider taking the
Lake Placid Olympic Site Tour. The package includes
admission to just about everything.

The **Olympic Center,** Lake Placid 12946, (518)
523–1655, is open year-round. For information on the
bobsled and luge rides, call (518) 523–4436. The
Summer Storm bobsled ride operates Wednesday
through Sunday from 10:00 A.M. until 12:30 P.M. and
from 1:30 until 4:00 P.M. The Summer Storm bobsled
ride costs $20. Winter rides, except for the "1-mile-one-
minute" bobsled ride, which costs $100 per person, are
available at $30 each. Call for winter hours.

It is surprising to drive north and find a spot near
Lake Placid and Saranac Lake whose principal connec-

tions are with events that occurred hundreds of miles from the Adirondacks. Here are the homestead and grave of the militant abolitionist John Brown, who was executed for his part in the 1859 raid on the U.S. arsenal at Harper's Ferry, Virginia. The homestead and grave are maintained today as the ◆**John Brown Farm State Historic Site.**

Brown and several of his sons had organized their followers to stage the raid in the hope that the captured arms might be used to launch a war of liberation on behalf of black slaves in the South. But his involvement in the abolitionist cause began years before the failed Harper's Ferry attack. His sons had home-

John Brown Farm

steaded in Kansas during the period in the 1850s when the territory earned the name "Bloody Kansas" because of the struggle to decide whether it would be admitted to the Union as a slave or a free state; Brown went to fight on the abolitionist side and took part in the desperate struggle at Osawatomie. But Brown wasn't a Kansan himself. Inasmuch as he had a permanent home during that turbulent period, it was his farm at North Elba, near Lake Placid. He had moved here in 1849 to participate in a plan to settle free blacks in an agricultural community called Timbucto. The benevolent scheme hadn't worked, but Brown still considered North Elba home and had requested that he be buried there. Two of his sons, killed at Harper's Ferry, are also interred at the farm, as are several of his followers, whose remains were moved here in 1899.

The farmhouse at the John Brown Farm State Historic Site, Route 73, Lake Placid 12946, (518) 523-3900, is open from late May through late October, Wednesday through Saturday, 10:00 A.M. to 5:00 P.M.; Sunday, 1:00 to 5:00 P.M. Also open Memorial Day, Independence Day, and Labor Day. The grounds are open all year. Admission is free.

At the ◆ **Hathaway Boat Shop,** Chris Woodward builds Adirondack guide boats using the same techniques that Willard Hanmer, one of the boat's original builders, used back in the 1930s. And he's making them in the same building. The boats—the style is indigenous to the region between Saranac Lake and Old Forge—are used for hunting and guiding. Chris also makes and sells paddles, seats, and oars and sells boat accessories. The shop, at 9 Algonquin Avenue

(Route 3), Saranac Lake 12983, (518) 891-3961, is open weekdays 9:00 A.M. to 5:00 P.M. or by appointment. Call ahead to make sure he'll be there.

It's a long way from the State of Bashkir on the western slope of Russia's Ural Mountains to the heart of the Adirondacks, but a strain of doughty little curly-haired horses have made the transition admirably. No one is sure when or how the Bashkir horses first came to this country. The breed was discovered at the turn of the century in the Great Basin area of Nevada, where they were being used on cattle ranches. Today there are fewer than 2,000 American Bashkir Curly horses in the world. But the folks at ✦ **Somewhere Farms** are confident that once people get to know the breed—durable, calm, intelligent, and extremely hardy—that will change.

Randall and Leslie Fisher, owners of the farm, are among only three dozen registered breeders of the Bashkir Curly in the country. And the name is appropriate; newly born foals and, in the winter, adult horses, *do* have curly hair.

The Fishers welcome visitors to Somewhere Farms in Bloomingdale 12913, (518) 946-7802. Call ahead to make sure they'll be home.

It's difficult to suggest that a forest preserve encompassing almost six million acres—roughly the size of the state of New Hampshire—is off the beaten path. But **Adirondack Park** encompasses some of the state's finest out-of-the-way attractions and offers some of its best opportunities to leave civilization behind. The park is a unique mixture of public and private lands. Approximately 130,000 year-round residents live in 105 towns and villages, but 43 percent of the total acreage is state owned, constitutionally protected, "forever-wild" land.

To best get a sense of the park, stop at one of the two **Visitor Interpretive Centers:** Paul Smiths VIC, Route 30, Paul Smiths 12970, (518) 327-3000; or Newcomb VIC, Route 28N, Newcomb 12852, (518) 582-2000. Both are open daily, year-round, from 9:00 A.M. to 5:00 P.M. except Thanksgiving Day and Christmas Day. Admission is free. If you're interested in camping at one of the 500 campsites spread over 48 islands on 3 of the Adirondack's most scenic lakes, request the brochure, "Camping in the New York State Forest Preserve."

The Adirondacks and, in fact, much of New York State were once the territory of the Iroquois Confederation. Perhaps the most politically sophisticated of all the tribal groupings of North American Indians, the Iroquois actually comprised five distinct tribes—the Mohawks, Senecas, Onondagas, Oneidas, and Cayugas—who were later joined by the Tuscaroras to form the "six nations" of the confederation. The history and contemporary circumstances of the Iroquois are documented in the ◈ **Six Nations Indian Museum,** a "living museum" that presents its material from a Native American point of view.

The museum—opened in 1954—was built by the Faddens, members of the Mohawk Nation, and is still operated and staffed by members of that family. The museum's design reflects the architecture of the traditional Haudenosaunee (Six Iroquois National Confederacy) bark house. The long house is a metaphor for the Confederacy, symbolically stretching from east to west across ancestral territory.

A visit to the museum—jam-packed with artifacts—is a reminder that for centuries before Europeans arrived the Iroquois were building a society. Throughout the season Native Americans visit to talk about their histories, cultures, and their people's contributions to contemporary society.

The Six Nations Indian Museum, Roakdale Road (County Route 30), Onchiota 12989, (518) 891–2299, is open daily from July 1 through Labor Day, 10:00 AM. to 6:00 P.M. and by appointment the rest of the year. Admission is $2.00 for adults and $1.00 for children.

Once a part of the corridor used by trading and war parties in the days of the French and Indians, the area around Plattsburgh, on Lake Champlain, had settled into a peaceful mercantile existence by the end of the eighteenth century. It was in Plattsburgh that the ◆ **Kent-Delord House** was built in 1797 by William Bailey. Following several changes of ownership, the house was purchased in 1810 by Henry Delord, a refugee from the French Revolution who had prospered as a merchant and served as a justice of the peace in Peru, New York, before moving to Plattsburgh. Delord remodeled the house in the fashionable Federal style of the era and moved in in 1811, thus beginning more than a century of his family's residence here.

Just three years after the Delords moved into their new home, the War of 1812 came to Plattsburgh in the form of a southward thrust by British forces along Lake Champlain. But the enemy was repelled later that month by the Delords' friend Commodore Thomas Macdonough in the Battle of Plattsburgh.

Aside from the wartime seizure of the house, the story of the Kent-Delord House might be that of any home of a provincial bourgeois family during the nineteenth century. The difference, of course, is that this house has survived remarkably intact. It offers a fine opportunity to see how an upper-middle-class family lived from the days just after the revolution through the Victorian age and, not incidentally, houses a distinguished collection of American portrait art, including the work of John Singleton Copley, George Freeman, and Henry Inman.

The Kent-Delord House Museum, 17 Cumberland Avenue, Plattsburgh 12901, (518) 561–1035, is open from noon to 4:00 P.M., with guided tours available Tuesday through Saturday at noon, 1:30 P.M., and 3:00 P.M. and by appointment. Admission is $3.00 for adults, $2.00 for students and senior citizens, and $1.00 for children under 12. The museum is closed during January and February.

◆ **Yarborough Square** carries the works of more than 175 artists and craftspeople from the United States and Canada. A large collection of pottery, including stoneware, porcelain, and raku, is on display, as are metal sculptures and handcrafted jewelry —everything from recycled glass to hand-dyed porcupine quills, wrought iron pieces, and candles. The gallery, which also represents several painters, is truly a North Country find. It's at 672 Bear Swamp Road, Peru 12972, (518) 643–7057, and is open daily from 10:00 A.M. to 6:00 P.M.

The **Old Red Barn,** on the banks of the Little Chazy River, is a cooperative of professional local artisans who make and sell everything from pottery to jewelry to quilts. The barn, on Route 22, West Chazy 12992, (518) 493–2217, is open from May to September 14, Friday to Sunday from 11:00 A.M. to 6:00 P.M. or by appointment.

WESTERN ADIRONDACKS

The ◆**Akwesasne Cultural Center** is dedicated to preserving the past, present, and future of the Akwesasne Mohawk people, whose history in the area dates back thousands of years. The museum houses more than 3,000 artifacts and an extensive collection of black-ash splint basketry; it also offers classes in traditional art forms such as basketry, quillwork, and water drums. The library houses one of the largest Native American collections in northern New York and includes information on indigenous people throughout North America.

Akwesasne Cultural Center, Route 37 (R.R. 1, Box 14C), Hogansburg 13655, (518) 358–2240, is open daily year-round except Sunday and major holidays. Call for hours. Suggested museum contribution is $2.00 for adults and $1.00 for children ages 5 to 16.

New York State, as was mentioned in the introduction to this book, was somewhat of a staging area for America's westward expansion during the last century. It thus seems fitting that the greatest chronicler of the West in painting and sculpture was a New Yorker, who grew up in the town of Ogdensburg on the St. Lawrence River halfway between Massena and Lake Ontario. His name was Frederic Remington, and a splendid collection of his work and personal effects is today housed in the ◆ **Frederic Remington Art Museum** in that community.

Born in 1861, Remington quit Yale at the age of nineteen and went west, where he spent five years garnering the experiences and images that would come across so powerfully in his paintings and sculpture. Success as an illustrator and later as a fine artist came after 1885; when Remington died suddenly following an operation in 1909, he was still riding the crest of his popularity. His wife moved from the Remington home in Connecticut in 1915 and settled in the artist's boyhood home of Ogdensburg, in a rented house that had been built in 1810. Mrs. Remington willed her husband's art collection, along with those of his own works in his possession at the time of his death, to the Ogdensburg Public Library, and five years after her own death in 1923, the museum exhibiting this collection was opened in the house where she had lived.

The Remington works housed in the museum include fifteen bronzes, sixty oil paintings, ninety watercolors, and several hundred pen-and-ink sketches. Selections of works from his own collection, among them paintings by Charles Dana Gibson and the American impressionist Childe Hassam, are also on display.

The Frederic Remington Art Museum, 303 Washington Street, Ogdensburg 13669, (315) 393–2425, is open from May 1 through October 31, Monday through Saturday, 10:00 A.M. to 5:00 P.M., and Sunday, 1:00 to 5:00 P.M. Closed legal holidays. Major renovations are scheduled to be completed in July 1997, but call ahead to verify hours. Admission is $3.00 for adults, $2.00 for children ages 13 to 16 and senior citizens, and free for children under 12.

Around the turn of the century, when Frederic Remington looked west for artistic inspiration, hotel magnate George C. Boldt turned instead to his native Germany. Boldt's creativity wasn't a matter of putting paint to canvas or molding bronze, however. He was out to build the 120-room ◆**Boldt Castle,** Rhineland-style, on one of the Thousand Islands in the St. Lawrence River.

Boldt, who owned the Waldorf-Astoria in New York and the Bellevue-Stratford Hotel in Philadelphia, bought his island at the turn of the century from a man named Hart, but that isn't why it is named Heart Island. The name derives from the fact that the hotelier had the island physically reshaped into the configuration of a heart, as a token of devotion to his wife, Louise, for whom the entire project was to be a monumental expression of his love.

Construction of the six-story castle and its numerous outbuildings began in 1900. Boldt hired masons, woodcarvers, landscapers, and other craftspeople from all over the world to execute details ranging from terra-cotta wall inlays and roof tiles to a huge, opalescent glass dome. He planned and built a smaller castle as a temporary residence and eventual playhouse, and he built an underground tunnel for bringing supplies from the docks to the main house. There were bowling alleys, a sauna, an indoor swimming pool—in short, it was to be the sort of place that would take years to finish and decades to enjoy.

But there weren't enough years left. Mrs. Boldt died suddenly in 1904, and George Boldt, heartbroken, wired his construction supervisors to stop all work. The walls and roof of the castle were by this time essentially finished, but crated fixtures such as mantels and statuary were left where they stood, and the bustling island fell silent. Boldt never again set foot in his empty castle, on which he had spent $2.5 million.

Boldt died in 1916, and two years later the island and its structures were purchased by Edward J. Noble, the inventor of Life Savers candy. Noble and his heirs ran the deteriorating castle as a tourist attraction until 1977, when it was given to the Thousand Islands Bridge Authority, which has, over the past eighteen years, invested $9 million in rehabilitation efforts to preserve the historic structure.

Boldt Castle, Heart Island, Alexandria Bay 13607, (315) 482-2520 or 800-8ISLAND is accessible via water taxi from the upper and lower docks on James Street in Alexandria Bay, as well as to tour-boat patrons departing from both the American and the Canadian shores. The Castle is open from mid-May through mid-October, daily from 10:00 A.M. to 6:00 P.M. For information call ahead, or write 1000 Islands International Council, P.O. Box 400, Alexandria Bay 13607. Admission is $3.75 for adults and $2.00 for children ages 6 to 12. Groups of twenty or more, senior citizens, and military personnel receive a discount.

If you find the most appealing aspect of George Boldt's heyday to be the sleek mahogany runabouts and graceful skiffs that plied the waters of the

Thousand Islands and other Gilded Age resorts, make sure you find your way to the ◆ **Antique Boat Museum** in Clayton. The museum is a freshwater boat lover's dream, housing slender, mirror-finished launches, antique canoes, distinctive St. Lawrence River skiffs, handmade guideboats—more than 150 historic small craft in all.

The Antique Boat Museum takes no sides in the eternal conflict between sailing purists and "stinkpotters," being broad enough in its philosophy to house a fine collection of antique outboard and inboard engines, including the oldest outboard known to exist. The one distinction rigidly adhered to pertains to construction material: All of the boats exhibited here are made of wood.

The Antique Boat Museum, 750 Mary Street, Clayton 13624, (315) 686-4104, is open from May 15 to October 15 daily, from 9:00 A.M. to 4:00 P.M. Admission is $6.00 for adults, with reduced rates for senior citizens, students, and children.

The international cooperation exemplified by the St. Lawrence Seaway and the peaceful coexistence that allows pleasurecraft to sail unimpeded along the boundary waters of the St. Lawrence River and Lake Ontario are things we take for granted today, but this state of affairs has hardly existed since time immemorial. Barely more than a century ago, the U.S. Navy kept an active installation at **Sackets Harbor Battlefield,** on Lake Ontario's Black River Bay, against the possibility of war with Canada. And during the War of 1812, this small lakeport actually did see combat between American and British forces.

At the time the war began, Sackets Harbor was not yet a flourishing American naval port and the site of a busy shipyard and supply depot. It was from here, in April 1813, that the Americans launched their attack upon Toronto; a month later the tables were turned when the depleted American garrison at the harbor was beleaguered by a British attack upon the shipyard. The defenders repulsed the attack but lost most of their supplies to fire in the course of the struggle.

Today's visitor to Sackets Harbor can still see many of the facilities of the old naval base, including officers' homes and sites associated with the 1813 battle.

Sackets Harbor Battlefield, 505 West Washington Street, Sackets Harbor 13685, (315) 646-3634, is open Memorial Day to early October, Wednesday through Saturday from 10:00 A.M. to 5:00 P.M. and Sunday from 1:00 to 5:00 P.M. Also open Independence Day and Labor Day. Grounds are open all year from 8:00 A.M. to sunset. Admission is $3.00 for adults and $1.00 for children.

The ◆ **American Maple Museum**, dedicated to preserving the history and evolution of the North American maple syrup industry, houses three floors of antique sugaring equipment, logging tools, and artifacts. There are replicas of a sugarhouse and a lumber camp kitchen, and a Hall of Fame. The museum hosts three all-you-can-eat pancake breakfasts a year—in February, May, and September—to raise funds. Call for dates.

The American Maple Museum, Route 812 (P.O. Box 81), Croghan 13327, (315) 346-1107, is open Friday, Saturday, and Monday, 11:00 A.M. to 4:00 P.M. from

Memorial Day to June 30; and daily except Sunday, 11:00 A.M. to 4:00 P.M. from July 1 to early September. Admission is $2.00 for adults and $1.00 for children ages 5 to 12.

The ◆ **North American Fiddler's Hall of Fame & Museum,** dedicated to "each and every fiddler who ever made hearts light and happy with his lilting music," preserves, perpetuates, and promotes the art of fiddling and the dances pertaining to the art. It displays artifacts and collects tapes of fiddlers, and since its inception in 1976, has inducted a new member (or members) into its Hall of Fame each year. The museum, across from Cedar Pines Restaurant, Motel, and Campground in Osceola, is open Sundays from 1:00 to 5:00 P.M. from Memorial Day through the first Sunday in October, during major events, and by appointment. For information contact Blair Buell (7620 Collins Street, Lowville 13367) at (315) 376–6732.

The 2,100-acre ◆ **Whetstone Gulf State Park,** built in and around a 3-mile-long gorge cut in the eastern edge of the Tug Hill plateau, provides one of the most spectacular scenic vistas east of the Rocky Mountains. Mostly undeveloped, the park has fifty-six wooded campsites, a picnic area along Whetstone Creek, a man-made swimming area, and several hiking and cross-country ski trails (one circles the gorge). A 500-acre reservoir above the gorge provides canoeing and fishing (it's stocked with tiger muskies and largemouth bass).

Whetstone Gulf State Park, RD #2, Lowville 13367, (315) 376–6630 or (315) 482–2593, is open year-round, with admission charged during the summer months.

Limited facilities are available in winter. To reserve a campsite call the New York State Campsite and Cabin Reservation Program at 1-800-456-CAMP.

Black River Canoe Rentals, R.R. 1, Box 296C, Waters Road, Lowville 13367, (315) 376-8587 or 376-8740, will help you plan your trip and provide travel maps. They're open daily, weather permitting, from May to October.

Over the years ◆ **Greystone Manor,** a limestone mansion built in 1803, has served as a tearoom, tavern, nursing home, and convalescent home for Canadian soldiers. Since 1973 it has been the home of Irving and Helen Post and one of the area's finer restaurants. Prices are moderate and offerings varied. Favorites such as shrimp scampi and teriyaki steak share the menu with appetizers such as deep fried alligator. There are also menus for children and for those with smaller appetites.

Greystone Manor, Route 26, Martinsburg 13404, (315) 376-7714, is open May 1 through October. Lunch is served Tuesday through Friday, 11:30 A.M. to 1:30 P.M. Dinner is served Tuesday through Saturday, 5:30 to 9:00 P.M., and Sunday, 1:00 to 7:00 P.M.

The man who built ◆ **Constable Hall** was presented with rather a generous birthright: four million acres of Adirondack wilderness. His father, William Constable, Sr., purchased the property with two other New York City capitalists/real estate speculators and ultimately became the principal owner and chief developer. He sold large tracts to European and American land companies and families from New England, launching the settlement of the north country. In 1819

William Constable, Jr., built a Georgian mansion patterned on a family-owned estate in Ireland, and five generations of the Constable family lived there until 1947, when the house became a museum. The original deed is just one of the family mementos displayed at the home, which still has many of it original furnishings.

Constable Hall, Constableville 13325, (315) 397-2323, is open daily except Monday from June 1 to October 15. Admission is $2.00 for adults and 50 cents for children.

The completion of our counterclockwise tour through the Adirondacks takes us east to a point just north of Utica, to the ◆ **Steuben Memorial State Historic Site,** in the foothills of the mountains. Frederick von Steuben was a Prussian officer who, at the age of forty-seven, emigrated to the United States in 1777 to help drill the soldiers of the Continental Army. His first assignment was a challenging one. He was sent to the American winter encampment at Valley Forge, where morale was flagging and discipline, in the face of elemental hardship such as hunger and bitter cold, was virtually nonexistent.

As might be expected of a good Prussian officer, von Steuben rose to the occasion. Washington's troops at Valley Forge might not have had boots, but they learned how to march in file, as well as proceed through the other elements of classic military drill and perform effectively with the eighteenth-century frontline weapon of choice, the bayonet. The German émigré even found time to write a masterful treatise on military training, *Regulations for the Order and Discipline of the Troops of the United States.*

Steuben Memorial

Having served as inspector general of the Continental Army until the end of the war, von Steuben was richly rewarded by the nation of which he had lately become a citizen. Among his other rewards was a New York State grant of 16,000 acres of land. Allowed to pick his own site, he chose the area partially occupied today by the Steuben Memorial State Historic Site and built a simple, two-room log house.

In 1936 the state erected a replica of von Steuben's house on a site located within the 50 acres it had recently purchased as his memorial (the drillmaster is buried beneath an imposing monument not far from here, despite his wish that he lie in an unmarked grave). The cabin is open to visitors. Encampments and historical interpretations reflecting the military life of the Revolutionary War soldier are held at the memorial, and docents are available to discuss the baron's life.

The Steuben Memorial State Historic Site, Starr Hill Road, Remsen 13438, (315) 831-3737, is open from late May to Labor Day, Wednesday through Saturday, 10:00 A.M. to 5:00 P.M.; Sunday, 1:00 to 5 P.M. Admission is free.

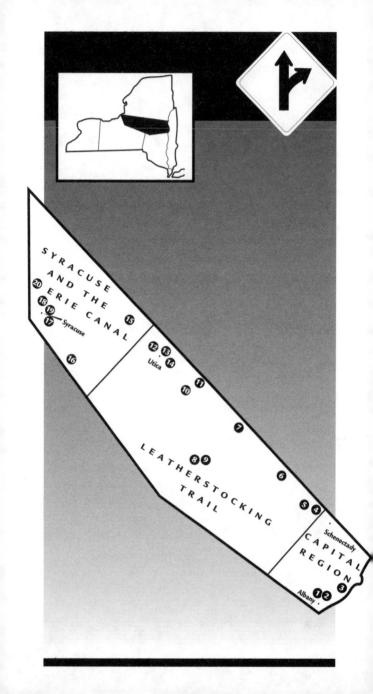

THE MOHAWK VALLEY

1. Albany Institute of History and Art
2. Schuyler Mansion State Historic Site
3. Waterford
4. Walter Elwood Museum
5. National Shrine of the North American Martyrs
6. Fulton County Museum
7. Fort Klock Historic Restoration
8. Fenimore House Museum and Farmers' Museum
9. Corvette Americana Hall of Fame
10. Remington Firearms Museum
11. Ace of Diamonds Mine and Campground
12. Children's Museum
13. Upstate New York Italian Cultural Center and Museum
14. Matt Brewing Company
15. Erie Canal Village
16. Lorenzo State Historic Site
17. L. and J. G. Stickley, Inc.
18. Erie Canal Museum
19. Everson Museum of Art
20. Octagon House

THE MOHAWK VALLEY

Drums along the Mohawk . . . Leatherstocking . . . "I had a mule and her name was Sal / Fifteen miles on the Erie Canal"—the lore of the Mohawk Valley has long been a part of the national consciousness. The reasons are plain: The valley has been an important highway between the East and the Great Lakes for centuries, and countless Americans have passed through here via Indian trails, the Erie Canal, Commodore Vanderbilt's "Water Level Route" of the New York Central railroad, and today's New York State Thruway. Here was where Jesuit missionaries met their end at the hands of the Iroquois, where James Fenimore Cooper's Deerslayer stalked, and where those who were to homestead the Midwest struck out along a water-filled ditch, in barges pulled by draft animals. Surely, this is one of the most storied corridors of the Republic.

Yet between Albany and Syracuse, there are plenty of places where people settled down to make things . . . guns in Ilion, pots and pans in Rome, gloves, as you might suspect, in Gloversville. They nevertheless left no shortage of open land, as you can see when you crest one of the gently rolling hills in the dairy country near Cooperstown. If you are coming from the East, what you see here is a harbinger of the next 1,500 miles. It isn't prairie yet, but the land is opening up, and the horizon is growing more distant. This is where midwestern vistas begin.

This chapter begins in Albany, very much an eastern city and the capital of New York State. From here the direction followed is east to west, corresponding closely to the route of the Mohawk River itself and, conveniently, the New York State Thruway.

CAPITAL REGION

The conventional, foursquare approach to Albany is by way of the public facade it presents—the massively beautiful and ornate State Capitol building, partly designed by H. H. Richardson, or the four monolithic, marble-clad state office towers so closely associated with the grandiose visions of the late Nelson Rockefeller. But in order to see a subtler side of the city and surrounding area and to learn more of its antecedents and historic persona than is revealed by those gargantuan examples of power frozen in masonry, visit the ◆ **Albany Institute of History and Art.** Descended from lyceums and art galleries that date back to 1791, the institute has followed an acquisitions policy geared to collecting art, decorative arts, and historical artifacts related to the art, history, and culture of Albany and the upper Hudson River Valley from the seventeenth century to the present.

Hudson River art, of course, means the Hudson River School, which is well represented here with works by painters such as Cole, Durand, and Cropsey. But the institute possesses fine examples of an even older regional genre, the sometimes-anonymous portraits of the Dutch burghers and their families who dictated the tone of Hudson Valley life during the seventeenth and eighteenth centuries. The Dutch in Holland had become the world masters of portraiture in the 1600s, as patrons and artists collaborated to compile a magnificent pictorial record of bourgeois life when the concept itself was still something new. It is fascinating to see how their New World counterparts worked a hundred years later. The experience is heightened by the institute's collection of early Hudson Valley furniture and silver, which formed the day-to-day surroundings of the people in the portraits.

The Albany Institute of History and Art, 125 Washington Avenue, Albany 12210, (518) 463-4478, is open Wednesday through Sunday, noon to 5:00 P.M. The galleries are closed on certain holidays. Admission is free on Wednesday; Thursday through Sunday, adults $3.00, seniors and students $2.00. Children 12 and under, free. Members are always free.

The Schuylers were among the earliest of the Dutch settlers of the upper Hudson Valley and were involved throughout the colonial period in trading, agriculture, land development, and local politics. The most renowned member of the family was Philip Schuyler (1733–1804), whose manorial home is today preserved as the ◆ **Schuyler Mansion State Historic Site.**

Although Albany has grown up around the mansion and deprived it of its once-rural hillside setting, it stands as a monument not only to its talented and versatile builders but also to the best in eighteenth-century taste.

Philip Schuyler designed the mansion himself in the Georgian style, with rose-colored brick walls, graceful fenestration, and double-hipped roof (the awkward hexagonal brick entry vestibule is an 1818 addition), and furnished it largely with purchases he made during a 1761–62 trip to England.

After Schuyler died in 1804, his house and much of the family land in Albany were sold and used as a private residence and later an orphanage. The Schuyler Mansion was acquired by the state in 1912, restored, and opened to the public.

The Schuyler Mansion is as fine a place as New York State offers to learn about life as it was lived among the most fortunate levels of society in the mid-1700s. The mansion is an architectural gem, and it houses an excellent collection of colonial- and Federal-period furnishings.

The Schuyler Mansion State Historic Site, 32 Catherine Street, Albany 12202, (518) 434-0834, is open April through October, Wednesday through Saturday from 10:00 A.M. to 5:00 P.M. and Sunday from 1:00 to 5:00 P.M.; November through March, by appointment only. Also open on Memorial Day, Independence Day, and Labor Day. Admission is $3.00 for adults, $1.00 for children 5 to 12, and $2.00 for New York State senior citizens.

One of Philip Schuyler's interests during his later years was the development of a canal and lock system in New York State. It was in the three decades after his death that canal building really hit its stride in the United States, turning formerly sleepy villages into canal boomtowns, involved in the lucrative trade between New York City and points west. Once such town is ◆ **Waterford,** located near Cohoes just upriver from Albany.

Founded by the Dutch as Halfmoon Point in the early 1620s at the point where the Mohawk River flows into the Hudson, Waterford was incorporated under its present name in 1794 and is today the oldest incorporated village in the United States. In 1799 it became the head of sloop navigation on the Hudson, but its glory days of commerce came later, in the 1820s, when the new Champlain and Erie canals made the town not merely a backcountry terminus but an important waystation and transfer point on a statewide transportation system.

Unfortunately for Waterford and many of its sister communities, not all major canal towns became major railroad towns after the iron horse ended the brief supremacy of the artificial waterways. Waterford did prosper as a small manufacturing center during the nineteenth century, however, and the legacy of this era is the village's lovely residential architecture, much of it in the regionally significant "Waterford" style characterized by Federal details and Dutch-inspired single-step gables. Such architectural distinctions have earned the village center a place on the National Register of Historic Places. The historic district is the subject of tours given during "Canalfest" the second Saturday of May each year. It features boat rides, hayrides, a boat show, a craft fair, food, and entertainment.

From April through October in the village center at Erie Canal Lock 2, a series of outdoor exhibits details the history of the 1823 canal and the present-day barge canal.

Waterford attractions outside the village center include the **Champlain Canal,** this section of which was dug in 1823 and is still filled with water; the **Waterford Flight,** a series of five locks on the still-operating New York State Barge Canal, whose 169-

foot total rise is the highest in the world; a state park at **Lock 6;** and **Peebles Island State Park. Waterford Historical Museum and Cultural Center,** 2 Museum Lane, off Saratoga Avenue, Waterford 12188, (518) 238-0809, is open weekends from 2:00 to 4:00 P.M. Admission is free.

LEATHERSTOCKING TRAIL

The ◆ **Walter Elwood Museum,** in a former school, offers a wonderful overview of the area's history as well as an eclectic collection of historical and natural objects. It isn't one of those musty little spots with a collection of shaving brushes and pewter dishes; among the 20,000 artifacts, which include the fossilized footprint of a Tyrannosaurus rex, is the earliest television set (on permanent loan from the Edison Museum in Menlo Park, NJ) and an exhibit depicting life in the Victorian era—a life-size home with four completely furnished rooms.

The museum, one of the few and one of the largest public-school owned museums in the country, is named for a local teacher who opened a museum and bird sanctuary in 1940 so students could study nature and wildlife.

The Walter Elwood Museum, 300 Guy Park Avenue, Amsterdam 12010, (518) 843-5151, is open weekends throughout the year, except legal holidays. Donations are welcome.

The Erie Canal and the feats of engineering that its building entailed are the focus of **Schoharie Crossing State Historic Site,** farther up the Mohawk, at Fort Hunter. Seven canal-related structures dating from three periods of the waterway's construction or expansion are preserved here and provided with interpretive displays that explain their use. The visitor center has an exhibit on the Erie Canal and information on the site and surrounding area. **Putnam's Canal Store,** at Yankee Hill Lock 28 on Queen Anne's Road (about 2.2 miles east of the visitor center), was built during the 1850s and served as a store along the enlarged Erie Canal for many years. It now houses an exhibit on Erie Canal stores. Guided walking tours of the site are given at 11:00 A.M. and 2:00 P.M. on Wednesday, Thursday, and Friday during the season. Mule-drawn guided wagon tours are given from 11:00 A.M. to 2:00 P.M. every Saturday in July and August.

Along the old canal towpath are views of modern-day barge traffic on the Mohawk River, the depth of which in this area allows it to be used as a link in the New York State barge canal system.

Schoharie Crossing State Historic Site, 129 Schoharie Street, P.O. Box 140, Fort Hunter 12069, (518) 829–7516, is open mid-May through October 31 and Memorial Day, Independence Day, and Labor Day, Wednesday through Saturday, 10:00 A.M. to 5:00 P.M., and Sunday, 1:00 to 5:00 P.M. The grounds are open all year during daylight hours. Admission is free.

Long before there were canals or barges in this part of New York State, the waters of the Mohawk and its tributaries were plied by the canoes of the Iroquois. The Mohawk Valley was the heart of the empire of the five nations, one of which was the tribe that gave the river its name. In what is today the town of Auriesville stood the palisaded village of Mohawk longhouses called Ossernenon in the seventeenth century; here, in 1642, a raiding party of Indians returned with three French and twenty Huron captives in custody. Among the French were a Jesuit priest, Isaac Jogues, and his lay assistant, Rene Goupil.

Goupil was tomahawked to death when his attempt to teach a child the sign of the cross was interpreted as the casting of an evil spell. Jogues was rescued by the Dutch during a Mohawk trading foray to Fort Orange, and he returned to Europe and eventually Quebec. But he volunteered to go back to Ossernenon in May 1646, as part of a group attempting to ratify a peace treaty with the Mohawks, and was captured near the village by a faction of the tribe favoring a continuation of hostilities. Both he and a lay companion, Jean Lalande, were murdered by tomahawk-wielding braves in October of that year. Canonized by the Roman Catholic church in 1930 along with five Jesuit missionaries martyred in Canada, Jogues, Goupil, and Lalande are honored at the ◈ **National Shrine of the North American Martyrs** in Auriesville.

The shrine, which occupies the hilltop site of the original Mohawk village of Ossernenon amid 600 verdant acres, is maintained by the New York Province of the Society of Jesus, the same Jesuit order to which Isaac Jogues belonged. Founded in 1885, the shrine accommodates 40,000 to 50,000 visitors each year during a season lasting from the first Sunday in May to the last Sunday in October. Mass is celebrated in the vast "Coliseum," the central altar of which is built to suggest the palisades of a Mohawk village; there are also a Martyrs' Museum, rustic chapels, and a retreat house.

For information on the schedule of observances at the National Shrine of the North American Martyrs, Auriesville 12016, call (518) 853–3033.

The French Catholic missionaries working among the Indians in the seventeenth century were not without their successes. The most famous name among Mohawk converts of that era is Kateri Tekakwitha, the "Lily of the Mohawks," born at Ossernenon and baptized at what is now the village of Fonda, where the **Fonda National Shrine of Blessed Kateri Tekakwitha** is now located. Maintained by the Conventual Franciscan Order, the shrine commemorates the life of the saintly Indian girl who lived half of her life here, before removing to the community of converted Indians established by the French at Caughnawaga, near Montreal, where she died in 1680 at the age of twenty-four. (In 1980, on the tercentenary of her death, Pope John Paul II announced the beatification of Kateri Tekakwitha, which is the last step before canonization in the Catholic church.)

Aside from its religious connections, the Fonda site of the Tekakwitha shrine is interesting because of its identification by archaeologists as the location of a Mohawk village, also called Caughnawaga. Artifacts dug from the village site are exhibited in the shrine's Native American Exhibit, located on the ground floor of a revolutionary-era Dutch barn that now serves as a chapel. Indian items from elsewhere in New York State and throughout the United States are also part of the exhibit.

The Fonda National Shrine of Blessed Kateri Tekakwitha, off Route 5, Fonda 12068, (518)

853-3646, is open daily, May through October from 9:00 A.M. to 4:00 P.M. Admission is free.

Just north of Fonda and nearby Johnstown is Gloversville, home of the ◆ **Fulton County Museum.** Gloversville was originally called Kingsborough, but the townspeople adopted the present name in 1828 in homage to the linchpin of the local economy in those days—tanning and glove making. It is the glove industry that provides the Fulton County Museum with its most interesting exhibits, housed in the Glove and Leather Room. Here is the state's only glove-manufacturing display—a complete, small glove factory of the last century, donated to the museum and reassembled in its original working format.

There is also a Weaving Room that demonstrates the technique from raw flax to the finished product; an Old Country Kitchen; a nineteenth-century Lady's Room, complete with costumes and cosmetics; a Country Store; an old-time Candy Store; an Early Farm display; and a Country Schoolroom. Be sure not to miss the Indian Artifact exhibit on the first floor.

The Fulton County Museum, 237 Kingsboro Avenue, Gloversville 12078, (518) 725-2203, is open May and June, Tuesday through Saturday, 10:00 A.M. to 4:00 P.M.; July and August, Tuesday through Sunday, noon to 4:00 P.M.; and September through mid-November, Tuesday through Saturday, 10:00 A.M. to 4:00 P.M. Admission is free.

Fate plays a capricious hand in deciding which industries a town will be noted for. Gloversville got gloves; Canajoharie, our next stop along the Mohawk, got chewing gum—specifically the Beech-Nut Packing Company, of which town native Bartlett Arkell was president in the 1920s. Because of Mr. Arkell and his success in business, Canajoharie also came into possession of the finest independent art gallery of any municipality its size in the United States—the **Canajoharie Library and Art Gallery.**

Arkell's beneficence to his hometown began with his donation of a new library in 1924. Two years later he donated the funds to build an art gallery wing on the library, and over the next few years he gave the community the magnificent collection of paintings that forms the bulk of the gallery's present holdings. Subsequent additions were made in 1964 and 1989.

This institution has become not merely an art gallery with a library attached but an art gallery with a small town attached. The roster of American painters exhibited here is astounding, totally out of scale with what you would expect at a thruway exit between Albany and Utica. The Hudson River School is represented by Albert Bierstadt (*El Capitan*), John Kensett, and Thomas Doughty. There is a Gilbert Stuart portrait of George Washington. The Winslow Homer collection is the third largest in the United States. The eighteenth century is represented by John Singleton Copley; the nineteenth, by luminaries such as Thomas Eakins, George Inness (*Rainbow*), and James McNeill Whistler (*On the Thames*). Among twentieth-century painters are Charles Burchfield, Reginald Marsh, and the painters of the Ash Can School: N. C. Wyeth and his son Andrew (*February 2nd*), Edward Hopper, Thomas Hart Benton, and even Grandma Moses.

There is also a Frederic Remington bronze, *Bronco Buster.* Add a collection of eighty Korean and Japanese ceramics, the gift of the late Colonel John Fox, and you have all the more reason—as if more were needed—to regard Canajoharie as a destination in itself rather than a stop along the way.

The Canajoharie Library and Art Gallery, 2 Erie Boulevard, Canajoharie 13317, (518) 673–2314, is open Monday through Wednesday, 10:00 A.M. to 4:45 P.M.; Thursday, 10:00 A.M. to 8:30 P.M.; Friday, 10:00 A.M. to 4:45 P.M.; Saturday, 10:00 A.M. to 1:30 P.M.; closed Sunday. Admission is free.

Art played little part in the life of the Mohawk Valley in the year 1750, when Johannes Klock built the farm-house-fortress preserved today as the ◆ **Fort Klock Historic Restoration.** Located above the river at St. Johnsville, Fort Klock is a reminder that the building of stout-walled outposts capable of being held defensively was by no means confined to the "Wild West" of the late 1800s. In 1750 the Mohawk Valley *was* the Wild West, and a man like Klock found it necessary to build a home that could serve just as easily as a fortress.

Like his neighbors at scattered sites along the river, Johannes Klock engaged in fur trading and farming. Canoes and bateaux could tie up in the cove just below the house, yet the building itself stood on high enough ground and at a sufficient distance from the river to make it easily defensible should the waters of the Mohawk bring foes rather than friendly traders. The stone walls of Fort Klock are almost 2 feet thick and are dotted with "loopholes" that enabled inhabitants to fire muskets from protected positions within.

Now restored and protected as a registered National Historic Landmark, Fort Klock and its outbuildings, including a recently restored Dutch barn, tell a good part of the story of the Mohawk Valley in the eighteenth century—a time when the hardships of homesteading were made even more difficult by the constant threat of the musket, the tomahawk, and the torch.

Fort Klock Historic Restoration, Route 5, St. Johnsville 13452, (518) 568-7779, is open from June through October, Tuesday through Sunday, 9:00 A.M. to 5:00 P.M. An admission fee is charged.

Thirty miles south of the Mohawk River is the origin of another of America's great waterways, the Susquehanna River at Otsego Lake. The village of Cooperstown lies at the southern end of 9-mile-long "Glimmerglass," so-named by James Fenimore Cooper, the American novelist whose family founded the village that is now synonymous with ultimate achievement in America's national pastime. The National Baseball Hall of Fame is what initially brings most visitors to Cooperstown, but once they arrive, many are delighted to find two other equally engaging museums.

The ◆ **Fenimore House Museum,** showcase for the New York State Historical Association, features changing exhibits of works largely from the eighteenth through early twentieth centuries, with an emphasis on paintings, early photographs, textiles, and other items relating to the American experience. Among the works are Hudson River School paintings by such luminaries as Thomas Cole and Asher B. Durand, folk art, and period furniture and paintings associated with Mr. Cooper.

Recently the museum added a $10 million, 18,000-square-foot wing to display The Eugene and Clare Thaw Collection of American Indian Art, with more than 700 masterpieces spanning 2,400 years that highlight the artistry of North America's indigenous peoples. The Great Hall features a selection of large-scale objects from regions throughout North America.

The museum, overlooking the lake, has a formal terrace garden and provides visitors with expansive views.

Just across the street is the ◆ **Farmers' Museum,** a cluster of historic building where the trades, skills, and agricultural practices of nineteenth-century rural New York State come to life. The museum's 1845 Village Crossroads is made up of ten early-nineteenth-century buildings all built within 100 miles of Cooperstown and moved here as life-size working exhibits. Among the buildings are a tavern, blacksmith's shop, one-room schoolhouse, and print shop. All are furnished period-style, and the museum interpreters perform the tasks appropriate to each building. Penny candy is sold at Todd's General Store. Lippitt Farmstead, a nineteenth-century house, barn, and outbuilding complex, presents farming practices of the day.

Among the special events are an old-time Fourth of July, the September Harvest Festival, and a Candlelight Evening at Christmastime that features sleigh rides and hot wassail.

The Farmers' Museum (607–547–1450) and the Fenimore House (607–547–1400) in Cooperstown

13326, are open April through December. Call for days and hours. Admission to either museum is $9.00 for adults and $4.00 for children ages 7 to 12. A Cooperstown Discovery Pass, which provides admission to both museums as well as the National Baseball Hall of Fame, is available. Call (507) 547–1410 for information.

Cooperstown, a place synonymous with baseball, also hosts a museum to its favorite car. In addition to memorializing the 'Vette, the ◈ **Corvette Americana Hall of Fame** immortalizes the memory of an era when Elvis was king, Marilyn Monroe was queen, and Tod and Buzz were the princes of Route 66.

Corvette Americana Hall of Fame

The museum functions as a time tunnel through the past forty years of American culture, and every display room—with an audio-video montage of slides, Top Forty musical hits, and film snippets— is a time capsule. Each car is built into its own Hollywood set featuring 12-foot by 30-foot photo murals of famous American landmarks.

Among the thirty-five cars displayed are a 1953 Corvette, a 1958 283/290 Fuelie, a 1982 Collector's Edition, and the Mako Shark II show car, displayed in an underwater setting complete with real sharks.

Corvette Americana Hall of Fame, Route 28, Cooperstown 13326, (607) 547–4135, is open daily March through December, 10:00 A.M. to 6:00 P.M., and July and August, 10:00 A.M. to 8:00 P.M. Admission is charged.

When the management of Rhinebeck's Beekman Arms (see page 35) decided to refurbish the inn's antique public rooms, they called on Tim and Eileen McCormack of **Waterwheel Woodworks at Dovetail Farms** to handcraft pieces that would look as authentic as the rest of the place. The cabinetmakers hand planed, pegged, and dovetailed each piece just as they do when they make any of their American primitive pieces.

Life at the circa 1810 Dovetail Farms also reflects an earlier time. In addition to handcrafting furniture, the McCormacks raise sheep, selling some of the fleece and weaving the rest into items to sell to passersby. They also sell organic lamb and pork.

Stop in for a tour of the woodworks, shop, and farm; visit the showroom; or just "set a spell" in one of the oak rockers.

Dovetail Farms, Christian Hill Road, Cooperstown 13326, (607) 293-7703, is open year-round. Tours are offered from May to November, Tuesday through Sunday, noon to 5:00 P.M. or by appointment.

Moon Dreams offers a serene respite from the hurly-burly of downtown Cooperstown. Patrons listen to soothing music as they browse among books, CDs, crafts, and jewelry. They're invited to linger in the shady garden or enjoy tea and light snacks and meals in the oak paneled Tea Room, where a reader will interpret Tarot cards or tea leaves. If visitors still feel stressed, the second floor of Moon Dreams houses counselors and therapists offering a wide variety of New Age therapies and alternative health counseling.

Moon Dreams, 137 Main Street, Cooperstown 13326, (607) 547-9432, is open daily.

It was an environment very much like the one depicted at The Farmers' Museum's Village Crossroads that produced one of the great American toolmakers, inasmuch as dependable firearms were indispensable tools of frontier life and westward expansion. In 1816 Eliphalet Remington was twenty-four years old and in need of a new rifle. He made a barrel at his father's village forge and then walked into the Mohawk Valley town of Utica to have it rifled (rifling is the series of twisting grooves inside a gun barrel that give the bullet spin—and therefore accuracy—and distinguish it from the smoothbore muskets of earlier days). He may not have known it then, but gun making was to be his life's work and the Remington Arms Company his creation. You can learn the history of America's oldest gun maker at the

◆ **Remington Firearms Museum** in Ilion, which houses an impressive collection of rifles, shotguns, and handguns dating back to Eliphalet Remington's earliest flintlocks. Here are examples of the first successful breech-loading rifles, for which Remington held the initial 1864 patents; rare presentation-grade guns; and company firsts including bolt-action and pump rifles, autoloading rifles and shotguns, and the Model 32 over-and-under shotgun of 1932.

Other displays include explanations of how firearms are built today, advertising posters and other firearms ephemera, and even antique Remington typewriters—yes, it was the same company.

Antique Double Derringer
Remington Firearms Museum

The Remington Firearms Museum, Catherine Street, off Route 5S, Ilion 13357, (315) 895-3200, is open Monday through Saturday, 9:00 A.M. to 4:00 P.M. From May through October the museum is also open on Sunday, 1:00 to 4:30 P.M. Admission is free.

"Herkimer diamonds," found just north of Ilion at Middleville, aren't really diamonds. Nor are they generally very valuable. But they're a load of fun to prospect for, and the ◆ **Ace of Diamonds Mine and Campground**—once known as the Tabor Estate, where the diamonds were first dug—can provide you with all the tools to begin your hunt.

The "diamonds" are really clear quartz crystals found in a rock formation called dolomite, buried ages ago. Surface water containing silicon seeped down through the earth and was trapped in pockets in the dolomite. Tremendous heat and pressure caused the crystals to form, and over the years erosion, weathering, and water have exposed the strata. The crystals at the Ace of Diamonds are found in pockets in the rock and in soil surrounding the weathered rock. They're primarily used for mineral specimens, but ones of gem quality are used in arts and jewelry.

Ace of Diamonds Mine and Campground, Route 28, Middleville 13406, (315) 891-3855 or 891-3896, is open April 1 through October 31 daily. There is a digging fee of $6.00 per adult and $2.00 for children 7 and under.

From Ilion it's just a short hop down the thruway to Utica and a pair of worthwhile museums. The **Munson-Williams-Proctor Institute** is the sort of thing small cities do well, given farsighted founders and the right endowment. The institute is a multifaceted operation that places a good deal of emphasis on community accessibility and service, with free group tours, a speakers' bureau, and children's art programs, as well as free admission and a modestly priced performing arts series (some performances take place at the nearby Stanley Performing Arts Center). But you don't have to be a Utica resident to enjoy the major holdings, which include a collection of paintings strong in nineteenth-century genre work and the Hudson River School, as well as moderns such as Calder, Picasso, Kandinsky, and Pollock; comprehensive art and music libraries; a sculpture garden; and even a children's room where patrons can leave their kids for supervised play while they enjoy the museum. Also on the grounds of the institute is **Fountain Elms,** a beautifully restored 1850 home in the Italianate Victorian style, which was once the home of the philanthropic Williams family. Four period rooms on the ground floor exemplify Victorian tastes. At Christmastime the house is resplendent with Victorian ornamentation.

The Munson-Williams-Proctor Institute, 310 Genesee Street, Utica 13502, (315) 797–0000, is open Tuesday through Saturday, 10:00 A.M. to 5:00 P.M., and Sunday, 1:00 to 5:00 P.M. Admission is free.

Having retrieved your little ones from the children's room at the institute, take them next to a museum of their own. Outside of New York City, Utica's ◆ **Children's Museum** is now the largest such institution just for kids in the state, having grown like Topsy since its founding by the city's Junior League.

Since 1980 it has occupied its own five-story, 30,000-square-foot building, which it keeps chock-full of participatory and hands-on exhibits concentrating on natural history, the history of New York State, and technology. Installations designed for children ages 2 to 12 and their families include a Dino Den; Childspace, for children from infant to 12; Iroquois longhouse and artifacts; a natural history center; and bubbles, architecture, and dress-up areas. The museum also offers special exhibitions on a monthly basis and special programs for children and their families on Saturdays beginning at 2:00 P.M., from October through July. Portions of the permanent Railroad Exhibit, which includes a Sante Fe dining car and diesel locomotive, are on display next to the museum.

The Children's Museum, 311 Main Street, Utica 13501, (315) 724–6128, is open year-round Tuesday through Sunday, 10:00 A.M. to 4:30 P.M. The museum is closed on most major holidays. Admission is $2.50 per person; members are admitted free.

Upstate New York's only Italian American museum, dedicated to the memory of all Italian immigrants, features an Immigrant Room with a photo exhibit, memorabilia, and artifacts; an art gallery for contemporary Italian American artists; and a Folk Art Room, with a regional doll collection. There's also a great little gift shop that carries gourmet Italian food items.

The ◆ **Upstate New York Italian Cultural Center and Museum,** 668 Catherine Street, Utica 13501, (315) 735–0336, is open Sunday from 1:00 to 4:00 P.M. For more information call the headquarters at (315) 684–9502.

In 1888 German-born F. X. Matt II opened a brewery in West Utica. Today the ◆ **Matt Brewing Company** is the second-oldest family-owned brewery—and twelfth largest—in the country. In addition to the Saranac family of beers, it also produces numerous specialty microbrews, including New Amsterdam and Harpoon.

And now the best news: You can tour the brewery and then sample the wares for free in the 1888 Tavern (the brewery makes an 1888 Tavern Root Beer for kids and teetotalers). The tour includes a visit to the seven-story brew house, the fermenting and aging cellars, and the packaging plant.

The Matt Brewing Company, 811 Edward Street, Utica 13502, (315) 732–3181, ext. 2234, is open for tours Monday through Saturday year-round. Advance reservations are recommended. Admission is $3.00 for adults and $1.00 for children ages 6 to 11. Free parking is available in the Tour Center Concourse at the corner of Court and Varick streets.

SYRACUSE AND THE ERIE CANAL

Hop aboard a horse-drawn canal boat at ◆ **Erie Canal Village,** which opened in Rome in 1973 near the site where the first spadeful of dirt for the Erie Canal was dug on Independence Day in 1817. The short-lived canal era may have been only a prologue to the age of the railroad—but in the 1820s New Yorkers thought the Erie Canal was one of the wonders of the world.

The *Chief Engineer,* which keeps to a regular schedule of thirty-five-minute trips on the restored section of the original canal at the village, was built of Mohawk Valley oak to the same specifications as the passenger-carrying packet boats of the canal's early years. The Harden Carriage Museum displays a varied collection of horse-drawn vehicles used on roads and snow. Other buildings in the village—nearly all more than a hundred years old and moved here from other communities in the area—include a tavern, church, smithy, canal store, settler's house, barn, and the New York State Museum of Cheese. The Erie Canal Museum explains the technological and social importance of the Erie Canal. Fort Bull, dating from the French and Indian Wars, is also on the premises.

The village presents historical craft demonstrations, interpretive programs, and seasonal festivals, with the primary focus on canal and harvest activities.

Erie Canal Village, Routes 49 and 46, Rome 13440, (315) 337–3999, is open daily, 9:30 A.M. to 5:00 P.M. from May 1 through Labor Day. Admission is charged. Boat rides are an additional $3.00 per person.

If a visit to the Erie Canal Village has brought you to Rome, stop in at the **Corning-Revere Factory Store.** The store offers terrific bargains on slightly irregular and factory-closeout items from the company's standard line of copper-clad stainless steel, as well as aluminum-slab stainless steel and copper-slab stainless steel. It also carries Corning Ware and other selected kitchen equipment.

The Corning-Revere Factory Store, 137 Liberty Plaza, Rome 13440, (315) 337–7828, is open Monday through Saturday, 10:00 A.M. to 6:00 P.M. and Sunday noon to 4:00 P.M.

Back before the Erie Canal was built, years before anyone thought of putting a copper bottom on a steel pot, this part of New York State was the western frontier, ripe for settlement, agriculture, and the development of manufacturing. During those first decades of American independence, land development companies operated much as they had in colonial times, securing rights to vast sections of virgin territory and undertaking to bring in settlers and get them started. One such outfit was the Holland Land Company, which in 1790 sent its young agent John Lincklaen to America to scout investment possibilities. Two years later he reached the area around Cazenovia Lake, between present-day Rome and Syracuse, and his enthusiasm for the area's prospects led his firm to invest in 120,000 acres here. A village, farms, and small businesses soon thrived, with Lincklaen remaining in a patriarchal and entrepreneurial role that demanded the establishment of a comfortable family seat. The result was Lincklaen's 1807 building of his magnificent Federal mansion, Lorenzo, today preserved at the ⬥ **Lorenzo State Historic Site.**

The little fiefdom of Lorenzo offers an instructive glimpse into why New York is called the Empire State. Lincklaen and the descendants of his adopted family, who lived here until 1968 (the same year that the house, with its contents, was deeded to the state), were involved with many of the enterprises that led to the state's phenomenal growth during the nineteenth century—road building, canals, railroads, and industrial development.

Lorenzo

The mansion, surrounded by twenty acres of lawns and formal gardens, sits on the shores of a 4-mile-long lake. It is rich in Federal-era furnishings and the accumulated possessions of a century and a half of Lincklaens. As of 1996 seven of the eight principal rooms and the central halls have been restored. The southwest bedroom was wallpapered with a reproduction of the original Jeffrey and Company of London paper, first hung in the room at the turn of this century. In the latest renovations, Zuber & Cie, in business in Rixheim, France, since the eighteenth century, used their original printing blocks to reproduce an 1870 paper originally hung in Lorenzo in

1901. These projects are part of an ongoing process to fully restore the site to its turn-of-the-century beauty.

Lorenzo State Historic Site, Route 13, Cazenovia 13035, (315) 655-3200, is open May 15 through October 31, Wednesday through Saturday and on Monday holidays, 10:00 A.M. to 5:00 P.M.; Sunday, 1:00 to 5:00 P.M. The grounds are open all year, 8:00 A.M. to dusk. Admission is $3.00 for adults and $1.00 for children.

Around the turn of the century, the aesthetic revolution called the Arts and Crafts Movement swept America. Its proponents rejected the superfluous ornamentation found in the popular Victorian furniture, advocating instead a return to simple ideas, honest craftsmanship, and sturdy construction. Gustav and Leopold Stickley, followers of the movement, began making Craftsman—also known as Mission—furniture.

Today Mission furniture is all the rage again, and cheap knockoffs can be found at discount stores throughout the country. But to see what the Stickleys had in mind, visit the company that continues to craft the same fine pieces that the brothers did at the turn of the century.

◆ **L. & J. G. Stickley, Inc.,** Stickley Drive, Manlius 13104, (315) 682-5500, offers tours Tuesday at 10:00 A.M.

At the beginning of the nineteenth century, a swamp northwest of Manlius became the site of Syracuse, which would be lifted to prominence by the salt industry and the Erie Canal, and which today contains the last of the "weighlock" buildings that once dotted the waterway. Built in 1850 in Greek Revival style, this weigh station for canal boats today houses the ◆ **Erie Canal Museum.**

Exhibits in the Weighlock Building, which houses the museum, include a 65-foot replica of a canal boat. The *Frank Buchanan Thomson,* named after a late museum director, offers a look at a typical Erie Canal vessel's crew quarters, immigrant accommodations, and cargo storage. Immigration along the canal is a special focus of the museum's exhibits, particularly with regard to its effects upon Syracuse. The museum experience also includes a hands-on display of canal equipment and explanations of the engineering involved in connecting Albany and Buffalo by means of a 363-mile artificial waterway, with eighty-three locks and eighteen aqueducts. The job wasn't easy, but the result was the longest and most successful canal in the world.

The Erie Canal Museum, 318 Erie Boulevard East, Syracuse 13202, (315) 471–0593, is open daily from 10:00 A.M. to 5:00 P.M.; closed holidays. Admission is free.

Having passed through the stages from swamp to canal boomtown to major commercial and industrial center by the end of the nineteenth century, Syracuse was ready for an art museum. The ◆ **Everson Museum of Art** was founded by George Fisk Comfort, a lion of the American art establishment who had been instrumental in establishing New York City's Metropolitan Museum and served as founder and dean of the College of Fine Arts at Syracuse University. Comfort organized the museum as the Syracuse Museum of Fine Arts, and in 1900 the first exhibition took place. A progressive policy toward acquisitions was in evidence even at that early date, with the initial show featuring, among older and more recognized masters, the work of impressionists such as Monet, Sisley, and Pissarro.

Renamed the Everson Museum in 1959 following a large bequest from the estate of Syracuse philanthropist Helen Everson, the museum moved in 1968 into its present quarters, a massive, modernist concrete structure that was architect I. M. Pei's first museum building. Its three exhibition levels contain nine galleries and a 50-foot-square, two-story sculpture court.

The Everson's holdings include anonymous colonial portraits (and one very famous and not so anonymous one of George Washington), the works of nineteenth-century genre and luminist painters, and paintings by twentieth-century names such as Robert Henri, John Sloan, Grandma Moses, Maxfield Parrish, Reginald Marsh, and Grant Wood. The museum possesses a good graphic art collection and a small but comprehensive photography section.

The emphasis at the Everson is heavily American. The museum's Syracuse China Center for the Study of American Ceramics houses the nation's premier collection in this field, with holdings dating from A.D. 1000 to the present. Here are pre-Columbian Native American vessels, colonial and nineteenth-century pieces, and contemporary functional and art pottery, as well as some 1,200 examples of ceramic craftsmanship from cultures outside the Western Hemisphere.

The Everson Museum of Art, 401 Harrison Street, Syracuse 13202, (315) 474–6064, is open Tuesday through Friday, noon to 5:00 P.M.; Saturday, 10:00 A.M.

to 5:00 P.M.; and Sunday, noon to 5:00 P.M. Admission is free, although a suggested donation of $2.00 is welcome.

If you've always wondered where salt comes from, visit the **Salt Museum** near Syracuse—"The City That Salt Built." At one time the area supplied the entire nation with the "white gold." The museum, constructed of timbers from former salt warehouses, explains the method of turning brine into salt, a process that ended in the 1920s.

The Salt Museum, Onondaga Lake Parkway, Liverpool 13088, (315) 453-6715, is open May through September, Tuesday through Sunday and Monday holidays, noon to 5:00 P.M. There is an admission charge for those over 15 years of age.

Bed & Breakfast Wellington, designed by Ward Wellington Ward, is a 1914 Arts and Crafts brick and stucco Tudor-style home with canvas flooring, an arched foyer, leaded glass windows, and tile insets. Rates range from $65 to $105, including private bath and breakfast. The B & B is at 707 Danforth Street in Syracuse, (315) 471-2433 or (800) 724-5006.

Although a visit to the ◆**Octagon House** is fascinating at any time of the year, springtime—when 300 bulbs come into bloom—is particularly beautiful. The exterior of the six-story, 1856 cobblestone house has been completely restored, and it has been furnished with antiques to make it look like Grandma will be in any minute to serve lemonade.

The Octagon House, 1 Milton Avenue, Camillus 13031, (315) 672-8334, is open Sundays and holidays from 1:00 to 5:00 P.M. and weekdays by appointment.

Call for a calendar of special events. Donations are welcome.

If your curiosity about canals has not yet been sated, you might want to sign on for a grand tour—a two- or three-day journey down the Cayuga-Seneca, the Oswego, the Champlain, and the Erie canals. **Mid-Lakes Navigation Company, Ltd.** offers escorted, navigated, and catered cruises, with departures from Buffalo, Syracuse, and Albany. During the day, passengers travel and dine aboard *Emita II*, a reconverted passenger ferry. At night the boat ties up on shore, and passengers check into a local hotel. It's a perfect blending of the nineteenth and twentieth centuries.

Lockmaster Hireboat
Mid-Lakes Navigation Company, Ltd.

The company also runs week-long bare-boat charters from Syracuse aboard European-style Lockmaster hireboats.

Mid-Lakes Navigation Company, Ltd., is headquartered at 11 Jordan Street, P.O. Box 61, Skaneateles 13152, (315) 685–8500 or (800) 545–4318.

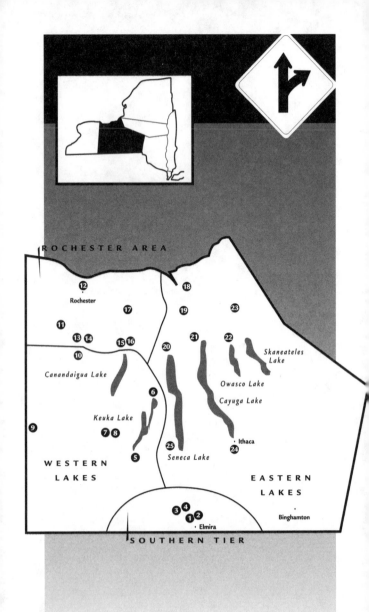

ROCHESTER AREA

⑫
Rochester

⑰

⑱

⑲

㉓

⑪

⑬ ⑭

⑮ ⑯

⑩

⑳

㉑

㉒

Skaneateles Lake

Canandaigua Lake

⑥

Owasco Lake

Cayuga Lake

Keuka Lake

⑦ ⑧

⑨

⑤

㉕

Seneca Lake

• Ithaca
㉔

WESTERN

LAKES

EASTERN

LAKES

③ ④
① ②

Binghamton

• Elmira

SOUTHERN TIER

THE FINGER LAKES

1. Mark Twain Study
2. National Soaring Museum
3. Ice Cream Works
4. Rockwell Museum
5. Glenn H. Curtiss Museum of Local History
6. Finton's Landing B & B
7. Vagabond Inn
8. Arbor Hill Grapery
9. Letchworth State Park
10. National Warplane Museum
11. Genesee Country Museum
12. Strong Museum
13. Ganondagan State Historic Site
14. Electronic Communication Museum
15. Granger Homestead and Carriage Museum
16. Sonnenberg Gardens
17. Historic Palmyra
18. Bonnie Castle Farm Bed & Breakfast
19. Grape Hill Gardens
20. Belhurst Castle
21. National Women's Hall of Fame
22. Cayuga Museum
23. D.I.R.T. Motorsports Hall of Fame & Classic Car Museum
24. Paleontological Research Institution
25. Watkins Glen State Park (Timespell)

THE FINGER LAKES

Here, between New York's "northern seaboard" along Lake Ontario and the Pennsylvania border, lies the region that many visitors consider to be the most beautiful part of the state. South of the Lake Ontario plain, the land appears to have been furrowed on a vast scale, with hilly farmland descending toward each of the Finger Lakes only to rise again before the next. The aptly named elongated lakes extend roughly north and south across an 80-mile swath of the state, offering vistas so reminiscent of parts of Switzerland that it's no wonder the city at the northern end of Seneca Lake was named Geneva.

Another distinctly European aspect of the Finger Lakes area is its status as New York State's premier wine-growing region. No longer limited only to the cultivation of native grape varieties, New York's vintners have come a long way, as visits to individual vineyards and the wine museum described below will demonstrate.

Scenes of well-tended vines in rows along steep hillsides may put you in mind of Europe, but the Finger Lakes region is rich in Americana. Here are museums of coverlets, Victorian dolls, and horse-drawn carriages. You'll even find Mark Twain's study and a museum devoted to Memorial Day.

We'll approach this area from the south, beginning near the Pennsylvania border and continuing up toward Rochester, then heading east along the New York State Thruway and the northern Finger Lakes.

THE SOUTHERN TIER

In the city of Elmira, there is a site with significant associations in the life of Mark Twain but one that many Americans—including Twain aficionados familiar with his haunts in Hannibal, Missouri, and Hartford, Connecticut—know little about. This is the ◆ **Mark Twain Study,** a charming little summer house on the campus of Elmira College.

Mark Twain married an Elmira woman named Olivia Langdon in 1870, and for many years the author and his family took leave of their palatial Hartford home to spend summers outside Elmira with Olivia's sister, Mrs. Theodore Crane. Mrs. Crane and her husband lived on a farm, where in 1874 they built Twain a freestanding octagonal study, with windows on all sides and a massive stone fireplace. Here Twain wrote *Tom Sawyer* and completed sections of *Huckleberry Finn, Life on the Mississippi, A Connecticut Yankee in King Arthur's Court,* and other works. It was, he said, "the loveliest study you ever saw."

Twain spent his last summer in Elmira in 1903 and returned the following year for his wife's funeral. The author himself was buried in Woodlawn Cemetery, on Walnut Street in Elmira, in 1910.

Difficult to maintain and protect from vandalism, the study was donated to Elmira College by the Langdon family in 1952, whereupon it was removed to its present site on the campus.

The Mark Twain Study, on the Elmira College Campus off Main Street, Elmira 14901, (607) 735-1941, is open mid-June to Labor Day, Monday through Saturday, 9:00 A.M. to 4:00 P.M., and on Sunday, 11:00 A.M. to 4:00 P.M. To arrange off-season visits write The Center for Mark Twain Studies, Quarry Farm, Box 900, Elmira College, Elmira 14901.

Head up Jerusalem Hill in Elmira to the **Hill Top Inn's** outdoor terrace for a great view of the Chemung Valley along with satisfying traditional cuisine. The Sullivan family has been greeting and feeding patrons since 1933. Hill Top Inn is open for lunch Monday through Friday, 11:00 A.M. to 2:00 P.M. and dinner nightly during the summer. Dinner is served Monday through Saturday, 5:00 P.M. to 10:00 P.M. the rest of the year. Closed some holidays. Reservations are recommended. Call (607) 732–6728.

The three-story Italianate mansion **Lindenwald Haus** has been a popular place to stay for more than 115 years. Innkeeper Camille Bodine is in charge of the seventeen renovated Victorian guest rooms. The 5-acre grounds are dotted with fruit trees; guests are welcome to walk, bike, or swim.

Lindenwald Haus, 1526 Grand Central Avenue, Elmira 14901, (607) 733–8753, is open year-round; call for information.

When Mark Twain's study was at its original site on the Quarry Farm belonging to his in-laws, it commanded a lovely view of the undulating hills along the Chemung River Valley. Little did Twain suspect that within a few decades after his death, these same hills would attract recreationists content not merely to walk the trails and pastures but instead to soar quietly far above them. By the 1930s Harris Hill, outside Elmira, had become the "Soaring Capital of

America." The science and sport of motorless flight is today kept vigorously alive at the ◆ **National Soaring Museum,** which offers visitors earthbound exhibits *and* the opportunity to go aloft in sailplanes piloted by experienced professionals.

Regardless of whether you agree with the museum's philosophy that soaring is "flying as nature intended," a visit to the facility offers a good introduction to this often-overlooked aspect of modern aviation. The museum houses the world's largest exhibit of contemporary and historic sailplanes, along with displays explaining the development of soaring and its relation to the parallel fields of meteorology and aerodynamics. You can even climb into a cockpit simulator, similar to those used to teach soaring, and learn what the experience of controlling a motorless plane is like.

Well, almost. To really understand soaring, you have to get off the ground. This can easily be arranged at the museum or at the Harris Hill Soaring Corp. Visitors' Center, which has a staff of competent pilots licensed by the FAA. Just check in at the Harris Hill Gliderport—the rides are available all summer long and on weekends throughout the year, weather permitting. Even if you don't go up yourself, it's fun to watch the graceful, silent flights and landings of the sleek sailplanes.

The National Soaring Museum, Harris Hill, RD 3, Elmira 14903, (607) 734-3128 (office) or 734-0641 (glider field), is open daily from 10:00 A.M. to 5:00 P.M. Call regarding schedules and cost of sailplane flights.

Upstream along the Chemung River is Corning, indelibly associated in most travelers' awareness with the Corning Glass Company and its Corning Glass Center and Museum and Steuben Glass Factory. If you'd prefer a more intimate environment in which to watch magnificent glass pieces being created by traditional glassblowing techniques, visit **Vitrix Hot Glass Studio** in Corning's historic Market Street district. Since 1959 Vitrix has been turning out some of the country's finest handblown glass pieces.

Vitrix Hot Glass Studio, 77 West Market Street, Corning 14830, (607) 936-8707, is open Monday through Friday, 10:00 A.M. to 6:00 P.M.; Saturday, 10:00 A.M. to 5:00 P.M.; and Sunday, noon to 5:00 P.M. Summers the studio stays open Monday through Saturday until 8:00 P.M.

Buffalo lays claim to chicken wings and beef on 'weck, and in the Chautauqua region goat's milk fudge is the regional delicacy. Now some folks in Corning hope to put the Finger Lakes on the map with wine ice cream. Mick Balock, co-owner of the ◆**Ice Cream Works,** invented the recipe and turned to Hunt Country Vineyards in nearby Branchport for product assistance: Foxy Lady wine ice cream was the result. As far as Mick knows, no similar recipe exists anywhere. The ice cream, hand-dipped or served through a soft-serve unit, has a subtle wine taste and is served in—you guessed it—a wine glass. The less adventurous can order up other ice cream house specialties such as Custer's Last Stand or a Sweet Ruthie at the authentically restored 1880s ice cream parlor.

The Ice Cream Works, West Market Street and Centerway Square, Corning 14830, (607) 962-8481, is open daily year-round, in summer from 9:00 A.M. to

10:00 P.M. and in winter from 11:00 A.M. to 5:00 P.M., serving food and desserts.

The ◆**Rockwell Museum** is an institution that owes its existence almost entirely to the single individual whose collection it comprises. Robert F. Rockwell is an area native and former proprietor of a small department store chain whose interest in western art dates to his youth spent on a Colorado ranch. He began collecting seriously in the late 1950s, over the years acquiring works not only by universally recognized masters of "cowboy" art such as Charles M. Russell and Frederic Remington but also by landscapists of the caliber of Albert Bierstadt and Thomas Hill and by animal artists A. F. Tait and Carl Rungius.

Rockwell's protean interests went beyond western art and sculpture to include an area dear to him as a Corning resident—the beautiful art glass created by Frederic Carder, cofounder of the Steuben Glass Works, which was later incorporated into Corning Glass Works, now Corning, Inc. Rockwell even collected antique toys.

By the beginning of the 1980s, Rockwell's collections, particularly of western art and Carder Steuben glass, were too extensive to be casually shown in his department stores and as part of exhibitions loaned to other institutions. He needed a museum, and one arrived in the form of Corning's old city hall, a Romanesque Revival structure built in 1893. The Corning Company acquired the building from the city for $1.00, renovations were undertaken, and in 1982 The Rockwell Museum opened. At present it houses the largest collection of western art on the East Coast, more than 2,000 pieces of Carder Steuben glass, Navajo weavings, antique firearms, Indian artifacts, and the toy collection as well.

The Rockwell Museum, Cedar Street at Denison Parkway, Corning 14830, (607) 937-5386, is open September through June, Monday through Saturday, 9:00 A.M. to 5:00 P.M.; Sunday, noon to 5:00 P.M. During July and August the hours are Monday through Friday, 9:00 A.M. to 7:00 P.M.; Saturday, 9:00 A.M. to 5:00 P.M.; and Sunday, noon to 5:00 P.M. The museum is closed Thanksgiving Day, Christmas Eve, Christmas Day, and New Year's Day. There is an admission fee.

WESTERN LAKES

The southern Finger Lakes region is a tranquil, easy-paced corner of the world that nevertheless nurtured one of twentieth-century America's great speed demons. At Hammondsport, on the southern tip of Keuka Lake, the ◆ **Glenn H. Curtiss Museum of Local History** chronicles the lifework of this native son, who was also a serious pioneer in motorcycling and aviation.

Glenn Hammond Curtiss started out, as did the Wright brothers, in the bicycle business. He quickly turned to motorcycles, building a V-8–powered bike on which he sped over 136 miles per hour in 1907. He also built engines that powered lighter-than-air craft, and in that same year he became involved with Dr. Alexander Graham Bell and other enthusiasts in the "Aerial Experiment Association." Curtiss's engineering helped lift the association's airplane *Red Wing* off the ice of Keuka Lake on the first public flight (as opposed to the Wrights' secret 1903 experiment) of a heavier-than-air craft in the United States.

Glenn Curtiss's accomplishments over the next twenty years dominated the adolescence of aeronautics. In 1910 he landed a plane on water for the first time, and in 1911 he became the first American to receive a pilot's license. In 1919 a Curtiss "flying boat" made the first transatlantic crossing by air. Meanwhile he had built his Curtiss Aeroplane and Motor Company into an industrial giant, employing 10,000 men at the peak of production during World War I. Sensing the traveling trends of the motor age, he even manufactured the first successful house trailers. Following a merger, the company became Curtiss-Wright, producer of World War II aircraft such as the Navy Helldiver and the P-40 of "Flying Tigers" fame. The museum, founded in 1960, houses seven historic aircraft and three reproductions, one of the latter is a flyable replica of the inventor's 1908 *June Bug.*

The Glenn H. Curtiss Museum of Local History, Route 54, one-half mile south of Hammondsport 14840, (607) 569-2160, is open from May 1 through October 31, Monday through Saturday, 9:00 A.M. to 5:00 P.M., and Sunday, 11:00 A.M. to 5:00 P.M.; from November 1 through April 30, it is open Monday through Saturday, 10:00 A.M. to 4:00 P.M., and Sunday, noon to 5:00 P.M. Admission is $4.00 for adults, $3.50 for senior citizens, $2.50 for students, and free for children ages 6 and under.

The Finger Lakes region is New York's wine country, and the area around Keuka Lake is in many ways its heart. It was along the shores of Keuka Lake that the late Dr. Konstantin Frank established his Vinifera Vineyards and proved to the world that the European grapes could survive New York State winters when grafted to hardy American rootstocks. Keuka Lake is also the home of Bully Hill Vineyards and the **Wine and Grape Museum of Greyton H. Taylor,** which recounts the story of a century and a half of wine making in New York State, particularly in the Finger Lakes area.

The Wine and Grape Museum of Greyton H. Taylor, G. H. Taylor Memorial Drive, Hammondsport 14840, (607) 868-4814, is open from May 1 through October 31, Monday through Saturday, 10:00 A.M. to 4:30 P.M.; Sunday, noon to 4:30 P.M. A moderately priced restaurant next door specializes in homemade pasta and dishes prepared with wine. The Bully Hill winery can also be visited for tours and tastings; call (607) 868-3210.

The Victorian **✦Finton's Landing Bed & Breakfast** overlooking Keuka Lake—nicknamed "the American Rhine"—was built in the 1860s as a steamboat landing for loading grapes harvested in the area. Today, the carefully restored, secluded inn, with a gazebo and L-shaped dock, has four guest rooms with private baths and a wraparound porch where a two-course breakfast is served (weather permitting). There's also a private beach.

Finton's Landing Bed & Breakfast, 661 East Lake Road, Penn Yan 14527, (315) 536-3146, is open year-round. The $79 rate includes breakfast.

If you're looking for seclusion—and magnificent mountain views—check out the **✦Vagabond Inn.**

The 7,000-square-foot inn stands in splendid isolation on top of a mountain in the Bristol range. Popular with honeymooners, the inn has a 60-foot-long Great Room with two massive fieldstone fireplaces, a Japanese garden, and an in-ground pool.

Don't be hasty in choosing a room: Each of the five has its special charms. For example, the Kimberly, which rents for $95 a night, has lots of windows that provide great views. The Bristol has its own fireplace, a Jacuzzi for two (with views of the mountains), and rents for $140. The Lodge, for $175, has a huge river-stone fireplace and hot tub chamber. Rates include breakfast.

The Vagabond Inn, 3300 Sliter Road, Naples 14512, (716) 554-6271, is open all year.

If you're visiting the area in late September, you might be just in time to sample one of the region's most unusual delicacies—Naples Grape Pie. Local bakeries produce more than 10,000 grape pies six weeks of the year, beginning with the start of the Annual Naples Grape Festival. If you're there any other time of the year, stop in for a slice at ◆ **Arbor Hill Grapery.** They serve them up all year, along with their wines and other wine food products, in a restored eighteenth-century building that once served as the local post office. They also serve light babecue-style lunches featuring wine soup, wine sausage, and—for dessert—hot grape sundaes.

Arbor Hill Grapery, 6461 Route 64, Bristol Springs (Naples) 14512, (716) 374-2870 or 374-2406, is open daily from May through December; weekends January through April.

At the southeast corner of the Alfred University campus is the **Stull Observatory,** considered to be one of the finest teaching observatories in the Northeast. It exists largely through the efforts of John Stull, who built or rebuilt all of the telescopes and many of the buildings. There are five major telescopes at the observatory: a 9-inch refractor dating from 1863, a 16-inch Cassegrain reflector, and 14-, 20- and 32-inch Newtonian reflectors.

The Stull Observatory at Alfred University, Alfred 14802, (607) 871–2208, offers public viewings (weather permitting) at the following times: September, October, November, February, March, and April, Friday from 9:00 to 11:00 P.M.; May, June, and July, Thursday from 10:00 P.M. until midnight. Admission is free.

The 14,350-acre ❖ **Letchworth State Park** along the Genesee River encompasses one of the most spectacular gorges and some of the most dramatic waterfalls in the East. It also encompasses the charming and elegant **Glen Iris Inn,** former home of William Pryor Letchworth, who began construction in 1859 and deeded the building and grounds to the state in 1907. Three meals are served daily at the inn, which has been restored and repainted in the colors of the 1890s. Rooms in the inn start at $70, and in the Pinewood Lodge (efficiency units a short distance from the inn) at $60. Reservations are recommended for meals and overnight stays. Call (716) 493–2622.

Letchworth State Park, Genesee State Park and Recreation Region, 1 Letchworth State Park, Castile 14427, (716) 493–3600, is open year-round. There is an admission fee to enter the park.

While at the park, tour the $25 million **Mount Morris Dam,** which in its first thirty-two years of operation has prevented damages estimated at $346 million. For information call (716) 658–4220.

Just west of Canandaigua Lake, the little town of Bristol has become renowned for pottery, hand-thrown and hand-decorated by "The Wizard of Clay," master potter Jim Kozlowski, and his assistants at **The Wizard of Clay Pottery.** Jim's production facilities and retail stores are housed in seven geodesic domes he designed himself.

The potter's wheel and eight kilns are in the work-shop. All pieces are fired at a temperature of 2,265 degrees F., which makes them extremely hard and durable, then treated with a specially formulated glaze that gives them a richly colored finish. The Wizard's most original pottery is decorated with delicate imprints from real leaves gathered from the Bristol hills.

The Wizard of Clay Pottery, Route 20A in Bristol, 3 miles east of Honeoye Lake (mailing address: 7851 Route 20A, Holcomb 14469), (716) 229–2980, is open daily from 9:00 A.M. until 5:00 P.M.

Heading northwest away from the Finger Lakes toward the Lake Ontario lowlands, we find the ◆ **National Warplane Museum** in Geneseo, dedicat-ed to the restoration and maintenance of flying-condi-tion World War II aircraft. The museum now has twen-ty-five aircraft in its collection dating from World War II and the Korean Conflict, including an ME-109 Messerschmitt, a Boeing B-17 Flying Fortress, and a Spitfire. Several of the planes, including the B-17, a

PBY 6-A Catalina, and a Fairchild C-119 Boxcar, are open to visitors for inspection.

If you're lucky enough to be in the area the third weekend of August, be sure to attend the "1941 Wings of Eagles" air show, featuring more than a hundred World War II–vintage aircraft.

The National Warplane Museum, Geneseo Airport, Geneseo 14454, (716) 243-0690, is open year-round, Monday through Friday, 9:00 A.M. to 5:00 P.M.; Saturday and Sunday, 10:00 A.M. to 5:00 P.M. Before going, call ahead—at times the aircraft may be off the field attending other air shows. Admission is $5.00 for adults, $4.00 for senior citizens, and $1.00 for children under 12.

ROCHESTER AREA

"Spend a day in the nineteenth century," reads the ◆ **Genesee Country Museum**'s invitation—but what's different about this reconstructed village in Mumford, on the southern outskirts of Rochester, is that the properties mean the *whole* nineteenth century, not just a small part of it. The fifty-plus buildings originally standing on, or relocated to, this site—all of them restored—represent virtually every stage of the development of upstate New York, from frontier days to late Victorian times.

The rail-fenced pioneer settlement reveals what rural living was like up near Lake Ontario around 1800. Just twenty-five years later the region had prospered to the extent that sumptuous Greek Revival homes such as Livingston Manor, also on the village grounds, could reflect the rapidly cultivated tastes of the upstate gen-

Richard Greeve's Kiowa
Genesee Country Museum

try. Turn the pages of another half-century, and you find the Victorian quirks and fussy comforts of the 1870 Octagon House, with its tidy cupola and broad verandas. Other village buildings include a carriage barn containing a collection of forty horse-drawn vehicles; a Gallery of Sporting Art, showcasing paintings and sculpture inspired by wildlife and the hunt; and the George Eastman birthplace, moved here in homage to the man who made nearby Rochester a "film capital" of an entirely different sort than Hollywood, California.

The Genesee Country Museum, off Route 36 in Mumford, (mailing address: P.O. Box 310, Mumford 14511), (716) 538–6822, is open from mid-May through mid-October: July and August, open daily, 10:00 A.M. to 5:00 P.M.; spring and fall, open daily, 10:00 A.M. to 4:00 P.M., except Monday. Admission is $10.00 for adults, $8.50 for senior citizens, $6.00 for children ages 4 to 16, and free for children 3 and under and museum members

If you picture a little girl in crinoline playing in the parlor of the Genesee Country Museum's Octagon House, you can well imagine the sort of dolls she might have for companions. Up near Rochester, in North Chili, Linda Greenfield has assembled a wonderful collection of these delicate and elaborately dressed playthings in her **Victorian Doll Museum.** The thousands of dolls at the museum not only reflect the tastes of the Victorian era but also show many types of doll construction that have faded from the picture in these days of molded plastic doll faces and bodies.

The Victorian Doll Museum premises are also the home of the **Chili Doll Hospital,** also run by Linda, who is an expert at doll restoration and repair. Antique dolls are appraised by appointment, and a collector's gift shop offers fine modern and period reproduction specimens.

The Victorian Doll Museum and Chili Doll Hospital, 4332 Buffalo Road, North Chili 14514, (716) 247-0130, are open Tuesday through Saturday, 10:00 A.M. to 4:30 P.M. from February through December, and Sunday, 1:00 to 4:00 P.M. November and December. Closed holidays. Admission to the museum is $2.00 for adults and $1.00 for children ages 12 and under.

"Please touch, feel, and explore" is the motto at one of the state's most unusual—and fun—museums. ◆ **Strong Museum,** the legacy of buggy-whip heiress Margaret Woodbury Strong, explores American life and tastes since 1820 with a variety of imaginative permanent and changing exhibits. Among them are one of the country's largest and best collections of Victorian furniture and an extensive display of antique dolls and dollhouses. To enter the exhibit "When Barbie Dated GI Joe: America's Romance with Cold War," visitors pass by a mock atom bomb shelter to interactive displays on space exploration, espionage, toys, games, and dolls. "UnEARTHing the Secret Life of Stuff: Americans and the Environment," explores the changing relationship between Americans and their environment by focusing on the familiar things we've created, used, and thrown away since 1850.

Among the exhibits most popular with children are: "One History Place," where original and reproduction artifacts from the turn of the century are arranged in settings that allow children to imagine life in the time of their parents and grandparents; and "Kid to Kid," which invites families to explore the theme of communication.

The Strong Museum, One Manhattan Square, Rochester 14607, (716) 263–2700 (Events Line: 716-454-7639), is open Monday through Saturday from 10:00 A.M. to 5:00 P.M. and Sunday from 1:00 to 5:00 P.M. Closed major holidays. Admission is $5.00 for adults; $4.00 for senior citizens and students with school I.D., and $3.00 for children ages 3 to 16. Under 3, free.

South and east of Rochester is a monument to another important development in the history of American popular culture: the shopping mall. Not the steel-and-glass malls of the 1950s, but a sturdy wooden structure erected in 1879. It was built by Levi Valentine as an all-purpose market and community center for the settlement he was developing, and thus it lays claim to being the first multistore "shopping center" in the United States. Today it houses the **Valentown Museum,** a collection of nineteenth-century small-town memorabilia that includes a reconstruction of the first railroad station in the Rochester area and a "Scientific Exhibition," which traveled around the country in a covered wagon from 1825 to 1880.

Valentown Hall, as Valentine called his "mall," had front doors opening into a general store, meat market, cobbler shop, barber shop, bakery, and harness shop. Upstairs were a grange lodge, rooms where classes in the arts and trades were held, and a community ballroom. The ambitious scheme lasted only thirty years, since the promised railroad connection never materialized (the restored station interior belonged to an earlier rail operation). The building was saved from demolition and restored in 1940 by J. Sheldon Fisher, a member of the Fisher family that gave its name to the town of Fishers, in which the hall is located. For information on when the museum can be visited, contact Mr. Fisher at the Valentown Museum, Valentown Square, Fishers 14453, (716) 924-2645.

"Ganondagan . . .a city or village of bark, situated at the top of a mountain of earth, to which one rises by three terraces. It appeared to us, from a distance, to be crowned with round towers." This is how M. L'Abbe De Belmont described a major town of the Seneca people, one of the five original Indian nations that have inhabited central New York since prehistoric times. A short time later the Governor General of New France led an army from Canada against the Seneca in an effort to eliminate them as competitors in the international fur trade.

The story of the Seneca people and the Iroquois (Haudenosaunee) Confederacy to which they belonged is recounted at ◈ **Ganondagan State Historic Site.** The site encompasses the palisaded granary M. L'Abbe De Belmont described, a sacred burial ground, and a system of trails. A twenty-seven-minute video in the visitor center relates the history of Ganondagan.

Ganondagan State Hisotric Site, 1488 Victor-Holcomb Road, Victor 14564, (716) 924-5849, is open

Wednesday through Sunday, 9:00 A.M. to 5:00 P.M., mid-May through the end of October. The trails are open all year. Admission is free except during special events.

Along with shopping malls, what could be more intrinsic to American civilization than the electronic media? The early days of our fascination with the vacuum tube (a device, young readers, that brought us our news, sports, and "Top 40" before the invention of the transistor) are chronicled in the Antique Wireless Association's ◆ **Electronic Communication Museum** south of the thruway in East Bloomfield. The museum's collections, housed in the handsome 140-year-old quarters of the East Bloomfield Historical Society, have been amassed by AWA members throughout the world. They include nineteenth-century telephones (in working order!), some of Marconi's original wireless apparatus, early shipboard wireless equipment, and the crystal radio sets that brought the first broadcast programs into American living rooms. A special attraction is a fully stocked replica of a circa 1925 radio store; another is wireless station W2AN, an actual broadcast operation staffed by AWA members.

The AWA Electronic Communication Museum, just off Routes 5 and 20 in East Bloomfield 14443, (716) 657-7489, is open May 1 to October 31, Sunday, 2:00 to 5:00 P.M.; also open Saturday, 2:00 to 4:00 P.M., and Wednesday, 7:00 to 9:00 P.M., during June, July, and August.

Preserved Americana seems to be the order of the day in this part of upstate New York, and the theme is carried along nicely at the ◆ **Granger Homestead**

and Carriage Museum in Canandaigua. *Homestead* is actually a bit too homespun a term for this grand Federal mansion, which must have been the talk of Canandaigua and all the farms around when it was built in 1816 by Gideon Granger, a lawyer who had served as postmaster general under Jefferson and Madison. Granger came here to spend the life of a country squire in his retirement, and his descendants lived here until 1930, when they willed many of the furnishings to Rochester's Memorial Art Gallery. The furnishings have been returned to the house on loan since it reopened in 1948. Nine restored rooms contain the furniture of the nineteenth century, including Federal, Empire, and Victorian styles. Decorative objects, original artworks, and China Trade porcelain are also displayed.

A distinctive attraction of the Granger Homestead is the Carriage Museum, which exhibits more than fifty horse-drawn vehicles made or used in western New York. The sociological implications of the various conveyances on display are explained in an informative exhibit titled "Sleighs and Surreys and Signs and Symbols."

The Granger Homestead and Carriage Museum, 295 North Main Street, Canandaigua 14424, (716) 394–1472, is open May through October. Guided tours are offered on the hour Tuesday through Saturday, 1:00 to 5:00 P.M., and also on Sunday, 1:00 to 5:00 P.M., in June, July, and August. Admission is $3.00 for adults and $1.00 for children.

◆ **Sonnenberg Gardens** are part of an estate built around a mansion representative of a much bolder and more expressive architectural aesthetic than Granger's Federal style—this is a Gilded Age extravaganza, part Tudor Revival, part Queen Anne, built in 1887 by Frederick Ferris Thompson, who founded the First National Bank of the City of New York. The forty-room mansion is well worth a tour—but even more impressive than the heavily carved Victorian furniture and fine Oriental rugs contained beneath the house's multicolor slate roof are the gardens themselves.

Frederick Thompson died in 1899, and in 1902 his widow, Mary Clark Thompson, began the extensive formal and informal plantings on the estate as a memorial to her husband. She worked at creating the

The Rose Garden
Sonnenberg Gardens

gardens for the next fourteen years and held occasional "public days" so that her Canandaigua neighbors (she had spent her youth in the town) could enjoy them as well. Since 1973 the gardens have been undergoing restoration, and they appear today much as they did during the first decades of the century.

What sets Sonnenberg Gardens apart is the sheer eclecticism. While many estates of the turn-of-the-century period were planted in a single style, usually formal French or the more naturalistic English, the gardens here represent just about every major mode of horticultural expression. There are a Japanese Garden, a rock garden, an Italian Garden, a sunken parterre display in a Versailles-inspired fleur-de-lis motif, an Old-Fashioned Garden, a garden planted entirely in blue and white flowers, and a Rose Garden containing more than 2,600 magnificent bushes blossoming in red, white, and pink. There are also a Roman bath, a thirteen-house greenhouse complex with a domed palm house conservatory, and fountains and statuary everywhere. After a while the mansion itself almost seems like an afterthought.

The Peach House, an informal restaurant in the greenhouse, is open daily in season from noon to 3:30 P.M.

Sonnenberg Gardens, off Route 21, Canandaigua, 14424 (716) 394–4922, is open daily mid-May through mid-October, 9:30 A.M. to 5:30 P.M. Admission is $7.50 for adults, $6.50 for senior citizens, and $3.00 for children ages 6 to 16. A season pass is available for $12.00.

The gracious 1810 **Morgan-Samuels Inn** nestled on forty-six acres of land, is a stone mansion with six bedrooms, ten fireplaces, three balconies, and a tennis court. Guests are served breakfast by candlelight. It's at 2920 Smith Road, Canandaigua 14424, (716) 394-9232. All rooms are under $100 a night.

One never knows where the nation's largest collection of this or that is going to turn up, but when it comes to coverlets, the answer is Palmyra.

The bed coverings displayed at the Alling Coverlet Museum, part of ◈ **Historic Palmyra,** were collected over thirty years by Mrs. Merle Alling of Rochester. Heirlooms all, they represent both the simple spreads hand-loomed by farmwives and the somewhat more sophisticated designs woven on multiple-harness looms by professionals during the nineteenth century. The collection also includes a number of handmade nineteenth-century quilts and antique spinning equipment.

The Alling Coverlet Museum (Historic Palmyra, Inc.), 122 William Street, Palmyra 14522, (315) 597-6737 or 597-4010, is open daily June through mid-September, 1:00 to 4:00 P.M.; also by appointment. Admission is free, although donations are welcome.

Another facet of Historic Palmyra is the **William Phelps General Store Museum.** Erected in 1826-28, this commercial building was purchased by William Phelps in 1868 and remained in his family until 1977. Having remained virtually unchanged over the past 125 years, the store, along with its stock, furnishings, and business records, amounts to a virtual time capsule of nineteenth- and early twentieth-century Palmyra. An unusual note: The gaslight fixtures in the store and upstairs residential quarters were used by a

Phelps family member until 1976, electricity never having been installed in the building.

The William Phelps General Store Museum, 140 Market Street, Palmyra 14522, (315) 597-6981 or 597-4173, is open June through September, Saturday, 1:00 to 4:00 P.M. Admission is free.

Historic Palmyra, Inc.'s final holding is the **Palmyra Historical Museum,** which was erected about 1900 as a hotel. It is now a museum housing a unique display of elegant furniture, children's toys and dolls, household items, tools, gowns, and other artifacts of bygone ages.

The Palmyra Historical Museum, 132 Market Street, Palmyra 14522, (315) 597-6981, is open June through September, Saturday, 1:00 to 4:00 P.M., and by appointment. Admission is free.

EASTERN LAKES

For a fabulous day of fishing, head for **Sodus Bay** on the shore of Lake Ontario. In season more than twenty-five charter boat companies offer their services in this small fishing paradise. Stop for a bite at **Papa Joe's Restaurant** on Sodus Point. The only restaurant open here year-round, it has a children's menu and entertainment on the deck on summer weekends. Lunch and dinner are served from 11:30 A.M. until 10:00 P.M. A two-bedroom apartment overlooking the bay is available for rent on a nightly basis. Call (315) 483-6372.

The lighthouse at **Sodus Bay Lighthouse Museum** (Sodus Point 14555, 315-483-4936) was built in 1871 and remained in use until 1901. Museum displays include: ship models, dioramas, shipboard equipment, a lens repair shop, and other maritime exhibits. There's a wonderful view of the lake from the tower. It's open May 1 through October 31, Tuesday through Sunday, 10:00 A.M. to 5:00 P.M. Donations are suggested.

The Victorian **Carriage House Inn** (corner of Ontario and Wickham Boulevard, 315–483–2100 or 800–292–2990), featured in Rand McNally's *The Best B & B's and Country Inns/Northeast,* charges $65 for a double room with a private bath, TV, and full breakfast. The stone carriage house overlooks the lake and lighthouse.

🏠 **Bonnie Castle Farm Bed & Breakfast,** on fifty acres of landscaped grounds overlooking Great Sodus Bay, is a three-story Victorian with private balconies and bilevel decks. Each of the eight rooms has its own bath and full kitchen. If you need three bedrooms, there's also an 1890 Victorian summer home—the Aldrich Guest House—whose balcony and porch overlook the water.

Bonnie Castle Farm Bed & Breakfast, 6603 Bonnie Castle Road, Wolcott 14590, (315) 587–2273 or (800) 587–4006, is open year-round. Rates range from $70 to $225 and include a full breakfast buffet (don't miss the appleknocker sausages).

One of the world's largest private lilac collections, featured in *Martha Stewart's Living* magazine (May 1996), is open for viewing during May and June at 🏠 **Grape Hill Gardens** in Clyde. Collections of magnolias, peonies, flowering crabs, and other herbaceous garden plants and flowering trees, all at varying stages of development, are also on display. The gardens, 1232 Devereaux Road, Clyde 14433 (315) 923–7290, are handicapped accessible and open daily from 8:00 A.M. to 8:00 P.M. in season. There is no charge for admission.

From coverlets to clocks . . . the northern Finger Lakes region seems to be New York State's attic, filled with interesting collections of things we might otherwise take for granted. In Newark the **Hoffman Clock Museum** comprises more than a hundred clocks and watches collected by local jeweler and watchmaker Augustus L. Hoffman. Housed in the Newark Public Library, the collection includes timepieces from Great Britain, Europe, and Japan, although the majority of the clocks and watches are of nineteenth-century American manufacture, with more than a dozen having been made in New York State. Each summer the museum's curator mounts a special exhibit devoted to a particular aspect of the horologist's art.

The Hoffman Clock Museum, Newark Public Library, 121 High Street, Newark 14513, (315) 331–4370, is open Monday, noon to 9:00 P.M.; Tuesday through Friday, 9:30 A.M. to 9:00 P.M.; and Saturday, 10:00 A.M. to 3:00 P.M. Closed Sunday and holidays. Admission is free.

Two of the Finger Lakes' most elegant inn-restaurants overlook its deepest lake, Seneca, in Geneva, the self-proclaimed "Trout Capital of the World."

It took fifty men more than four years to build the turreted red Medina stone ◆ **Belhurst Castle.** When finally completed in 1889, the cost of construction exceeded $475,000. Today the Richardsonian Romanesque inn has a reputation as one of the finer places in the region to stay and/or dine.

There are eleven guest rooms in the castle (including one with a private balcony and one, in the castle turret, with a widow's walk) and several houses on the grounds behind the castle. Locust Cottage, twenty minutes from the main complex, has its own private beach. Rates range from $65 off-season for a room in the castle to $980 for a seven-day, high-season stay at the cottage. Continental breakfast is included.

Dinner entree prices range from $19 to $27 and include unusual offerings such as scallopini of ostrich and petite filets of Russian wild boar tenderloin. More traditional offerings include chateaubriand and rack of lamb. A less expensive fixed-price menu is available weekdays (except holidays) until 6:30 P.M. Sunday brunch includes more than fifty items plus complimentary Bloody Marys and mimosas. Reservations are recommended for all meals.

Belhurst Castle, Lochland Road (Route 14), Geneva 14456, (315) 781-0201, is open year-round. Lunch and dinner are served daily.

"An oasis, a little island of beauty, peace, and friendliness in a busy world" is how **Geneva on the Lake** describes itself. The inn, with its terra-cotta tile roof, Palladian windows, Ionic columns, classical sculptures, and magnificent formal gardens, was built in 1910 by Byron Nester, who was inspired by the summer residences around northern Italy's lakes Garda and Maggiore. All rooms are suites and range in price—depending on time of year—from $162 to $481 for a night's stay. Rates include wine, fresh fruit and flowers, a wine and cheese party on Friday evening, and continental breakfast, weather permitting, on the terrace overlooking the gardens and lake.

Lunch is served on the terrace daily, except Sunday, from mid-June to early September; candlelight dinners with live musical entertainment are served Friday, Saturday, and Sunday evenings; and an elegant brunch is served Sunday.

Geneva on the Lake, 1001 Lochland Road, Route 14S, (P.O. Box 929), Geneva 14456, (315) 789–7190, is open all year.

"To honor in perpetuity these women, citizens of the United States of America, whose contributions to the arts, athletics, business, education, government, the humanities, philanthropy and science have been the greatest value for the development of their country." Thus were the parameters for entry outlined when the women of Seneca Falls created the ◆ **National Women's Hall of Fame** in 1969, believing that the contributions of American women deserved a permanent home.

And, indeed, the list of members reads like a "Who's Who": Marian Anderson, Pearl S. Buck, Rachel Carson, Amelia Earhart, Billie Jean King, Sally Ride, Dorothea Dix, and a host of others who have left their mark on American history and the American psyche.

Exhibits, housed in the bank building in the heart of the Historic District II, include a panel celebrating Elizabeth Cady Stanton, who led the way to rights for women, and artifacts and mementos about the members, events, and activities significant to women's history.

The National Women's Hall of Fame, 76 Fall Street, Seneca Falls 13148, (315) 568-8060, is open from May through October, daily from 9:30 A.M. to 5:00 P.M.; November through April, Wednesday through Saturday, 10:00 A.M. to 4:00 P.M., and Sunday, noon to 4:00 P.M. Closed Thanksgiving, Christmas, and New Year's days. Admission is $3.00 for adults, $1.50 for senior citizens and students, and $1.00 for children over 5. There is a family rate of $7.00.

Once a stop on the Underground Railroad, the **Hubbell House Bed & Breakfast** overlooking Van Cleef Lake was built in the 1850s as a Gothic Revival cottage and later enlarged and remodeled in the Second Empire style. The result is a delightfully eccentric building with scrolled bargeboards, wooden pinnacles, windows of all sizes, and a rear mansard roof with diamond-shaped slate tiles. It's furnished with an eclectic mix of antiques, including an 1860s Eastlake dresser, armchair, and rocker.

Hubbell House Bed & Breakfast, 42 Cayuga Street, Seneca Falls 13148, (315) 568-9690, is open all year. Rates, which include a full breakfast, range from $70 to $85 a night.

For a small town, Waterloo is large on preserving history and has two museums well worth a visit. It was in the village of Waterloo, in the summer of 1865, that a patriotic businessman named Henry C. Welles put forward the idea of honoring the soldiers who fell in the Civil War by placing flowers on their graves on a specified day of observance. On May 5 of the following year, thanks to the efforts of Welles and Civil War veteran General John B. Murray, the village was draped in mourning, and a contingent of veterans and towns-people marched to the local cemeteries and, with appropriate ceremonies, decorated their comrades' graves. Thus Memorial Day was born.

In 1966 President Johnson signed a proclamation officially naming Waterloo the birthplace of Memorial Day. On May 29 of that same Memorial Day centennial year, Waterloo's **Memorial Day Museum** was opened in a reclaimed mansion in the heart of town. The twenty-room, once-derelict brick structure is itself a local treasure, especially distinguished by the ornate ironwork on its veranda. Although built in the early Italianate Revival era of 1836–50, the house is being restored to its appearance circa 1860–70, the decade of the Civil War and the first Memorial Day observances.

The museum's collections cover the Civil War and the lives and era of the originators of the holiday, as well as memorabilia from all other U.S. wars.

The Memorial Day Museum, 35 East Main Street, Waterloo 13165, (315) 539-0533, is open Memorial Day weekend, July, and August, Mondays and Thursdays, 1:00 to 4:00 P.M., and Saturdays, 10:00 A.M. to 2:00 P.M. Admission is by donation. Tours are given by appointment.

Just a block from the Memorial Day Museum is the **Terwilliger Museum,** where the "antique and elegant" combine with the "long-lasting and functional" to tell the story of Waterloo and surrounding areas. The collection includes everything from Native American artifacts to Roaring Twenties fashions. Authentic full-size vehicles and a replica of a general store offer a slice of life as it used to be; and five rooms, decorated down to the last detail, each depict a specific era.

The Terwilliger Museum, 31 East William Street, Waterloo 13165, (315) 539-0533, is open all year, Monday from 2:00 to 5:00 P.M. and Wednesday from 7:00 to 9:00 P.M. Admission is by donation. Tours are given by appointment.

Some institutions have a pinpoint focus; others follow a more eclectic pattern of acquisiton and education. Occasionally, a small institution finds its focus as it matures, as is the case with the ◆ **Cayuga Museum** in Auburn, which is really two museums in one.

Founded in 1936, the Cayuga Museum contains the rich history of both Auburn, "the village that touched the world," and Cayuga County. Exhibits include business timekeeping devices, including the "Thousand Year Clock," manufactured by Auburn's Bundy brothers, whose Binghamton, New York, operation evolved into IBM. There's also an exhibit on the early history of the now-giant corporation. Other notables from Cayuga County who are highlighted at the museum include President Millard Fillmore; E. S. Martin, founder of the original, pre-Luce *Life* magazine; prison reformer Thomas M. Osborne; and Ely Parker, the Seneca Indian who penned the surrender at Appomattox.

In 1911 Theodore W. Case proved that recording sound on film was possible, and in late 1922 he made it a reality with the assistance of E. I. Sponable. Newly restored in 1993 after being forgotten for sixty years, the **Case Research Lab Museum** opened its doors to the public on the second floor of the Cayuga Museum's carriage house in June of that year. Exhibits include the laboratory building, the sound stage, and many examples of the early history, inventions, and laboratory equipment developed to commercialize sound on film. One of the museum's newest acquisitions is a 1928 REO Speedwagon panel truck.

The Cayuga Museum and the Case Research Lab Museum, 203 West Genesee Street, Auburn 13621, (315) 253-8051, are open Tuesday through Sunday from noon to 5:00 P.M., and Monday holidays. Admission is free, but a donation is welcome.

Classic cars, historic race cars, racing memorabilia—they're all exhibited at the ◆ **D.I.R.T. Motorsports Hall of Fame & Classic Car Museum,** along with a "Hall of Fame" of legendary race car drivers.

Among the classic cars on display are a 1926 Duesenberg, the 1929 Dodge Roadster that won first place in a Cross Country race in 1993, and a 1969 Dodge Charger Hemi 4-speed. For stock car enthusiasts, there's the Buzzie Reutimann "00" coupe, which won the first two Schaefer 100's, and "Batmobile" #112 driven by Gary Balough in 1980. In the Jack Burgess Memorial Video Room the "master of the microphone" recounts exciting racing events of the past. The Northeast Classic Motorsports Extravaganza is held each August.

Also here is Cayuga County Fair Speedway, home of Drivers Independent Race Tracks (D.I.R.T.), the second-largest race-sanctioning body in the nation (races every Sunday night May through September).

D.I.R.T. Motorsports Hall of Fame and Classic Car Museum, Cayuga County Fairgrounds, Route 31, Weedsport 13166, (315) 834-6667, is open daily April through December; closed January through March. Call for hours and admission rates.

Just south of Auburn at Emerson Park on Owasco Lake is the **Owasco Teyetasta,** a museum of the Northeast Woodland native peoples who first dwelled in what is now Cayuga County. Operated by the Cayuga Museum, the facility counts among its exhibits artifacts of the native peoples, as well as the skeleton of a 12,000-year-old woolly mammoth.

The Owasco Teyetasta, Route 38A, adjacent to Emerson Park, Owasco Lake 13130, (315) 253–8051, is open Memorial Day to Labor Day, Thursday through Sunday, noon to 4:00 P.M. Admission is free, but a donation is welcome.

In England, Americans Victoria and Richard MacKenzie-Childs worked for a small pottery shop, taught art, and designed and made clothing for stage and street wear. When they returned here, they opened **MacKenzie-Childs, Ltd.,** a multifaceted design studio and factory where more than 150 workers turn out handcrafted, hand-painted giftware including Majolica, glassware, linens, and floor cloths—all done, according to the couple, "within the elegance of a gentlemanly nineteenth-century estate . . . in an atmosphere of ethics, order, and grace."

MacKenzie-Childs, Ltd., Aurora 13026, (315) 364–7123, showroom and shop are open Monday through Saturday, 10:00 A.M. to 5:00 P.M. Studio tours are given Monday through Friday at 10:00 A.M. There is a fee for the tour.

Beaver Lake Nature Center is an Onondaga County park incorporating several different ecosystems, all connected by 9 miles of well-maintained hiking trails. A 200-acre lake, offering beautiful vistas but no recreational facilities, is a migration-time magnet for up to 30,000 Canada geese. Guided canoe tours of the lake are available during the summer; rental canoes are available for these tours, and you must preregister. The entire center is a great place for birders; more than 180 species have been sighted here over the years. The informative Beaver Lake Visitor Center is the starting point for a regular schedule of hour-long guided tours of the trails, given by professional naturalists each weekend.

Beaver Lake Nature Center, 8477 East Mud Lake Road, Baldwinsville 13027, (315) 638-2519, is open all year, daily, 7:30 A.M. to dusk. Admission is $1.00 per car and $10.00 per bus. Call ahead to register for guided group nature tours.

Ithaca, home to Cornell University, is also home of the ◈ **Paleontological Research Institution (PRI),** which houses more than two million fossils, one of the premier collections in the Western Hemisphere. The institution, located in a former orphanage on the southwest shore of Cayuga Lake, was founded by Gilbert D. Harris, a professor of geology at the university from 1894 to 1934.

Among the fossils exhibited are single-celled microfossils, ancient plants, the remains of ancient vertebrates such as dinosaurs and woolly mammoths, and a magnificent 425-million-year-old trilobite.

PRI, 1259 Trumansburg Road, Ithaca 14850, (607) 273-6623, is open Monday through Friday from 9:00 A.M. to 4:00 P.M. Tours are offered Mondays from 1:00

Paleontological Research Institution (PRI)

to 4:00 P.M. and the second Saturday of every month from noon to 4:00 P.M. There is no admission fee, but donations are gratefully accepted.

Stand on a ledge deep inside Watkins Glen Gorge as state-of-the-art technology—laser images, panoramic sounds, and special effects—transport you from the gorge's beginnings 4½ billion years ago, through the ice age, to the arrival of the people of the Seneca Nation.

The dramatic outdoor sound and light show, ◆ **Timespell,** is held in Watkins Glen State Park nightly from mid-May through mid-October. The show begins at 9:15 P.M. through early September and at 8:00 P.M. from early September until closing.

Admission for Timespell, in Watkins Glen State Park, Watkins Glen 14891, (607) 535–4960 or (800) 853–7735, is $5.25 for adults and $4.50 for children ages 6 to 11 and senior citizens.

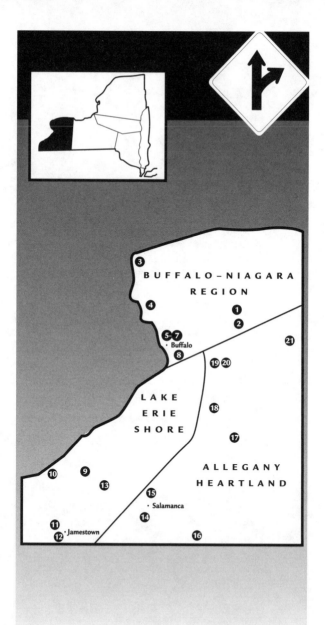

THE NIAGARA-ALLEGANY REGION

1. Iroquois National Wildlife Refuge
2. Asa Ransom House
3. Old Fort Niagara
4. Herschell Carrousel Factory Museum
5. Theodore Roosevelt Inaugural National Historic Site
6. Q-R-S Music Rolls
7. Burchfield-Penney Art Center
8. Pedaling History Bicycle Museum
9. Stockton Sales
10. McClurg Museum
11. Chautauqua Institution
12. Roger Tory Peterson Institute of Natural History
13. Lock, Stock & Barrel Country Store
14. Allegany State Park
15. B & B Buffalo Ranch
16. Rock City
17. Arcade and Attica Railroad
18. Pipe Creek Farm B & B
19. The Roycroft Inn
20. Toy Town Museum
21. Wyoming

THE NIAGARA-ALLEGANY REGION

Ever since the Erie Canal was opened a century and a half ago, New York City and Buffalo have assumed a front door–back door status in New York State. New York City became the Empire State's gateway to the world, a capital of international shipping and finance. The docksides and rail yards of Buffalo, meanwhile, were the portals through which the industrial output and raw materials of the Midwest flowed into the state. Buffalo became an important "border" city between the East Coast and the hinterlands, a center of manufacturing and flour milling whose fortunes have risen and fallen with the state of the nation's smoke-stack economy.

But don't write Buffalo off as an old lunch bucket town that gets too much snow in the winter. Buffalo has some impressive architecture, from Louis Sullivan's splendid Prudential Building and the art deco City Hall downtown to the Frank Lloyd Wright houses described below. South Park, with its conservatory, and Riverside Park on the Niagara offer welcome open spaces, and there are even culinary treasures like Buffalo chicken wings and beef on 'weck (hot sliced roast beef on a pretzel-salt-coated kimmelweck or kaiser roll).

The countryside at the western tip of New York provides further evidence as to why Niagara Falls isn't the only reason to drive to the end of the thruway. The Pennsylvania border country boasts giant Allegany State Park, a hiking and camping paradise, and the byways along the Lake Erie shore wander through a picture-pretty territory dotted with vineyards, cherry orchards, and roadside stands selling delicious goat's milk fudge. Yes, goat's milk fudge. It's the little serendipities that make traveling fun.

BUFFALO-NIAGARA REGION

Just to mix things up a bit, we'll venture out into the sticks to begin our tour of the Niagara-Allegany region. Only 40 miles northeast of Buffalo is a pristine tract of some 19,000 acres, the core of which (11,000 acres) makes up the federal ◆**Iroquois National Wildlife Refuge.** On either side of the refuge are the **Oak Orchard** (east) and **Tonawanda** (west) **Wildlife Management Areas,** operated by the state of New York's Department of Environmental Conservation. Both the Oak Orchard and the Tonawanda areas are primarily wetlands, with plenty of access trails on high ground, that offer superb opportunities not only for hunters (during designated seasons) but for hikers and birders as well.

The best time for birders to visit Tonawanda and Oak Orchard is from early March to mid-May. That's when more than 100,000 Canada geese, along with lesser numbers of black, pintail, and mallard ducks, American wigeon, teal, and shoveler and ringnecked ducks, pause on their northward migration, with some staying to nest. The transitional habitat along the borders of the marsh attracts shore and wading birds and migrating spring warblers.

The Iroquois National Wildlife Refuge headquarters, 1101 Casey Road, Alabama 14003, (716) 948-5445, is open Monday through Friday from 7:30 A.M. to 4:00 P.M. There are self-guided exhibits and an observation tower at the Oak Orchard Education Center on Knowlesville Road, just north of the town of Oakfield. The center is open daily from sunrise to sunset and is the starting point for four nature trails. For additional information contact the regional wildlife manager of the New York State Department of Environmental Conservation, 6274 East Avon-Lima Road, Avon 14414; (716) 226-2466.

The ⬥**Asa Ransom House** is an 1853 farmhouse on the site of one of the country's early gristmills. Several of the nine guest rooms have fireplaces and/or private front porches and balconies. The inn serves a "country dinner," with specialties such as raspberry chicken and smoked corned beef with apple raisin sauce, Sunday through Thursday, and a five-course fixed-price dinner Saturday. Lunch is served Wednesday and afternoon tea is served Thursday from 2:00 to 4:00 P.M. The inn and restaurant are closed Friday.

The Asa Ransom House is at 10529 Main Street, Clarence 14031, (716) 759-2315. A double room, including full breakfast, ranges from $89 to $145 Sunday through Thursday, with MAP available. A Saturday stay with MAP ranges from $190 to $260.

Thirty Mile Point Lighthouse, more than 60 feet high, was built of hand-carved stone near the mouth of Golden Hill Creek in 1875 to warn vessels of the sandbar and shoals jutting out into Lake Ontario. Visitors can climb the circular steel staircase to the top of the tower for magnificent views of the lake and

Canada. The lighthouse, now part of **Golden Hill State Park,** is free to those who pay a park entrance fee. It's open weekends and holidays from Memorial Day to Labor Day, 2:00 to 4:00 P.M. Lower Lake Road, Barker 14012, (716) 795-3885.

It seems as if it isn't possible to tick off too many miles in this state without encountering one of the string of forts that once defended the thirteen colonies' northwestern frontier and played so prominent a role not only in the struggles between the British and the French for North American supremacy but in our own War of Independence as well. The westernmost of these (in New York, at least) is ◆ **Old Fort Niagara,** located in Fort Niagara State Park downstream from Niagara Falls at the point where the Niagara River flows into Lake Ontario.

Fort Niagara occupies what was, in the days of conventional warfare, one of the most strategic locations in all of the interior of North America. The great "French Castle" erected here in 1726 served as the core of Fort Niagara's defenses through nearly a century of intermittent warfare and was in use as officers' housing as recently as World War I. Now restored to its eighteenth-century appearance, it is the focal point of Old Fort Niagara.

Restored between the years 1927 and 1934, the older buildings of Fort Niagara are maintained by the nonprofit, private Old Fort Niagara Association in cooperation with the state of New York. Beyond the silent military structures are broad vistas of Lake Ontario and, in clear weather, the rising mists of Niagara Falls 14 miles to the south.

Old Fort Niagara, Fort Niagara State Park, Youngstown 14174, (716) 745-7611, is open daily, July 1 through Labor Day, 9:00 A.M. to 7:30 P.M.; during the rest of the year, although daily opening is at 9:00 A.M., seasonal closing times vary. Closed Thanksgiving, Christmas, and New Year's days. During the summer there are frequent costumed reenactments of military drills, with musket and cannon firings. Admission is $5.75 for adults, $4.75 for senior citizens, and $3.50 for children ages 6 to 12.

Drummer at Old Fort Niagara

Scotland native Allan Herschell literally carved a place for himself in America's history when, in 1883, he produced the first steam-driven "riding gallery"—known today as a merry-go-round. By 1891, one machine a day was being shipped to places around the world; later the Herschell-Spillman Company became the world's largest producer of carousels and amusement park devices. And because merry-go-rounds need music, North Tonawanda also became a major producer of band organs.

The ◆ **Herschell Carrousel Factory Museum,** housed in an historic factory building, traces the history of Mr. Herschell, his hand-carved wooden animals, and the finished carousels. There are ongoing woodcarving demonstrations, and best of all for all us kids, an antique, hand-carved wooden carousel to ride. "Super Sunday" family performances are held at 2:00 P.M. from mid-June through mid-September.

The Herschell Carrousel Factory Museum, 180 Thompson Street, North Tonawanda 14120, (716) 693–1885, is open April through mid-June, Wednesday through Sunday, 1:00 to 5:00 P.M.; July and August, daily from 11:00 A.M. to 5:00 P.M.; and September through November, Wednesday through Sunday, 1:00 to 5:00 P.M. Closed major holidays. Admission is $4.00 for adults and $1.50 for children ages 2 to 12 and includes one carousel ride. Extra rides cost just 25 cents.

Heading upriver (or more likely, down Route I–190) we pass Niagara Falls and come to the terminus town of the Erie Canal and gateway to the Midwest. For a quick introduction to this sprawling inland port, head downtown to reconnoiter the city and Lake Erie from the twenty-eighth-floor observatory of **City Hall** (open weekdays from 9:00 A.M. to 3:00 P.M.) and then visit the nearby historic neighborhood of **Allentown.**

The works of a number of important architects and the homes of several famous people are tucked into the compact Allentown neighborhood. Representative of the district's myriad building styles are the Kleinhans Music Hall on Symphony Circle, designed in 1938 by Eliel and Eero Saarinen; the 1869 Dorsheimer Mansion, 434 Delaware Avenue, an early work of the peerless Henry Hobson Richardson; Stanford White's 1899 Butler Mansion (672 Delaware) and 1895 Pratt Mansion (690 Delaware); and a lovely example of the Flemish Renaissance style at 267 North Street. As for the haunts of the famous, there are the childhood home of F. Scott Fitzgerald, 29 Irving Street; the home of artist Charles Burchfield (once a designer for a Buffalo wallpaper company) at 459 Franklin Street; and, at 472 Delaware Avenue, the carriage house belonging to the now-vanished house occupied circa 1870 by the editor and part-owner of the *Buffalo Morning Express,* a man who hated Buffalo—Samuel Langhorne Clemens, whom we met back in Elmira under the name of Mark Twain. For information call the Allentown Association at (716) 881-1024.

One house in the Allentown neighborhood stands above all others in historic importance. For fifty years the home of prominent Buffalo lawyer Ansley Wilcox, the Greek Revival house at 641 Delaware Avenue became part of American legend on September 14,

1901, when a vigorous young man who had just rushed from a vacation in the Adirondacks stepped into the library to take the oath of office as president of the United States. William McKinley was dead, the victim of an assassin; the era of Theodore Roosevelt was about to begin.

The story of that fateful day and the tragic event that preceded it is told at the ◆ **Theodore Roosevelt Inaugural National Historic Site,** as the Wilcox House has been known since its restoration and opening to the public in 1971. Perhaps the most interesting aspect of the tale concerns the mad dash Roosevelt made from the Adirondacks to Buffalo. He had gone to the city and stayed for a few days at the Wilcox House after McKinley was shot by an anarchist at the Pan-American Exposition but had left to join his family at their mountain retreat after being assured by the president's doctors that his condition had stabilized. Notified several days later of McKinley's worsening state, the vice president made an overnight journey by horse and wagon to the nearest train station, where he learned that the president was dead. Roosevelt and his party then raced to Buffalo in a special train. Within two hours after his arrival, he was standing in Wilcox's library, wearing borrowed formal clothes as he took the oath of office as the nation's twenty-sixth president.

The Theodore Roosevelt Inaugural National Historic Site, 641 Delaware Avenue, Buffalo 14202, (716) 884-0095, is open Monday through Friday, 9:00 A.M. to 5:00 P.M.; weekends, noon to 5:00 P.M. It is closed on Saturday, January through March. Closed January 1, Good Friday, Memorial Day, July 4, Labor

Day, Thanksgiving Day, Christmas Eve, and Christmas Day. Admission is $3.00 for adults and $1.00 for children under 14.

The residential neighborhoods north of the downtown and Allentown areas of Buffalo boast five examples of the work of America's greatest architect, Frank Lloyd Wright. Wright's residential architecture is generally distributed within the central and upper Midwest, where he brought his "prairie style" to maturity. The fact that there exists a pocket of the master's work in Buffalo is due to his having designed a house in Oak Park, Illinois, for the brother of John D. Larkin, founder of the Larkin Soap Company of Buffalo. Larkin liked his brother's house and brought Wright to Buffalo to design the company headquarters. The Larkin Building, a light, airy masterpiece of commercial architecture, stood on Seneca Street from 1904 until it was unconscionably demolished in 1950. But fate was kinder to the five Buffalo houses built for Larkin Soap Company executives following Wright's arrival in town, all of which survive to this day. Here is a list of the **Frank Lloyd Wright houses** in Buffalo and their locations:

· **William Heath House,** 76 Soldiers Place, corner of Bird Avenue, completed in 1906 and landscaped by Frederick Law Olmsted. (Private; not open to visitors.)

· **Darwin D. Martin House,** 125 Jewett Parkway, corner of Summit Avenue. Also completed in 1906, this expansive home was unfortunately left vacant for seventeen years prior to the mid-1950s, during which time half of the original Wright windows were lost. It was restored in 1970 by the State University of New York at

Buffalo, which uses it for offices. For information regarding tours contact the School of Architecture and Planning, Hayes Hall, 125 Jewett Parkway, Buffalo 14214; (716) 831–3485.

· **George Barton House,** 118 Summit Avenue, a smaller brick structure with distinctive top-story casement windows and a broad roof overhang built in 1903–4. (Private; not open to visitors.)

· **Gardener's Cottage,** Martin Estate, 285 Woodward Avenue. Constructed in 1906, the cottage is one of the few surviving service buildings of the Martin Estate. (Private; not open to visitors.)

· **Walter Davidson House,** 57 Tillinghast Place. With the exception of Darwin Martin's 1926 summer house, built south of the city on a bluff above Lake Erie, the 1909 Davidson House is the last of Wright's Buffalo residences. (Private; not open to visitors.)

From what we know about Frank Lloyd Wright, we can surmise that if he ever caught a client putting a player piano in one of his houses, he would have rapped him across the knuckles with his walking stick. But the perennially old-fashioned machines began to flourish during the first decade of the twentieth century, when Wright was designing his radically modern houses, and they are with us still. Nowadays the most complete line of rolls for player pianos is manufactured and sold by a Buffalo institution called ◈ **Q-R-S Music Rolls.**

Q-R-S is one of the last (and also the oldest) manufacturers of player-piano rolls in the United States, having been founded in 1900 by Melville Clark, the man who perfected the player. During the heyday of the instrument in the 1920s, Q-R-S had plants in New York, Chicago, and San Francisco, but by 1966 only a small facility in the Bronx remained. A new owner bought the company and moved it to Buffalo, where subsequent ownership has kept it.

A piano-roll company like Q-R-S doesn't stay in business simply by cranking out reprints of "Sweet Adeline" and "You Are My Sunshine." Today you can buy rolls for Disney's "Hunchback of Notre Dame" or Whitney Houston's latest hit, and other tunes penned long after your player was built.

But not all player pianos are antiques. The company is making a device that will enable any piano to play music programmed on special Q-R-S CDs. You can order a copy of the company's current catalog through the mail, but if you're in the area it's a lot more fun to stop in at the factory and make your purchase after taking a tour.

Q-R-S Music Rolls, 1026 Niagara Street, Buffalo 14213, (716) 885–4600, is open Monday through Friday, 9:00 A.M. to 4:00 P.M., with a morning tour at 10:00 A.M. and an afternoon tour at 2:00 P.M. Admission fees, refunded with a purchase, are $2.00 for adults and $1.00 for children.

Just minutes from downtown the **Buffalo Museum of Science** houses an extensive collection of natural science exhibits. The museum was built in the 1920s and features a blend of classic dioramas and modern museum exhibitry. A stunning glass-enclosed atrium connects the museum to the Charles R. Drew Science Magnet School, one of the first science magnet schools in the nation to be physically and programmatically linked to a museum.

The museum's main exhibit hall is filled with exciting temporary exhibitions. A visit to the permanent "Dinosaurs & Co." exhibit provides an exciting look at some of the favorite prehistoric giants. "Insect World" features insects six times life-size in two vastly different ecosystems—the cloud forest in the coastal Andean highlands of north central Venezuela and the Niagara frontier region of New York State. Two halls of space provide detailed information about our world and the worlds around us; and observatories provide views of stars, planets, and our sun. The museum also features exhibits on endangered species, zoology, flora and fauna, gems and minerals, and technology.

The Buffalo Museum of Science is located at 1020 Humboldt Parkway (Best Street exit of the Kensington Expressway), Buffalo 14211; (716) 896–5200. Open Tuesday through Sunday from 10:00 A.M. to 5:00 P.M. Closed January l, July 4, Thanksgiving Day, and Christmas Day. Admission is $5.25 for adults and $3.25 for children, students, and senior citizens.

The Buffalo Museum of Science also operates **Tifft Nature Preserve** just 3 miles from downtown. Billed as an "Urban Nature Sanctuary," the preserve is a 264-acre habitat for animal and plant life, dedicated to environmental education and conservation. With miles of hiking trails, three boardwalks, and a self-guided nature trail, it's a wonderful place to spend the day hiking or fishing. For birdwatchers there's a 75-acre freshwater cattail marsh with viewing blinds. In winter the preserve rents snowshoes. Free guided nature walks are given every Sunday at 2:00 P.M. The

Makowski Visitor Center has some wonderful exhibits on ecology, animals, and plant life.

The Tifft Nature Preserve and Makowski Visitor Center, 1200 Fuhrmann Boulevard, Buffalo 14203, (716) 825-6397 or 896-5200, is open Tuesday through Sunday from 9:00 A.M. to 5:00 P.M. Closed January 1, Thanksgiving Day, December 24, and December 25. There is no admission charge.

The ◆ **Burchfield-Penney Art Center** exhibits the largest and most comprehensive collection of the works of Charles E. Burchfield, one of the country's foremost watercolorists, as well as the works of other western New York artists. The center, which serves the community as a multifaceted cultural and educational institution, also hosts numerous special exhibitions throughout the year.

One of the center's exhibits, "Access to Art," uses a unique assortment of interpretive tools such as hands-on art activities, interviews with artists, tactile works, and library resources to give visitors of all ages the skills to enjoy a museum without feeling intimidated.

The Burchfield-Penney Art Center, Rockwell Hall, Buffalo State College, 1300 Elmwood Avenue, Buffalo 14222, (716) 878-6012, is open Tuesday through Saturday from 10:00 A.M. to 5:00 P.M. and Sunday from 1:00 to 5:00 P.M.; closed Monday and major holidays. A $3.00 voluntary admission is collected at the door.

Cemeteries are not often thought of as places to go to for fun, but **Forest Lawn** is not a typical cemetery; it's more like a city park. The final resting place of prominent Buffalonians such as Red Jacket, the Seneca orator, and Millard Fillmore, the country's thirteenth president, is also a nature sanctuary, with 6,000 trees and 157 species of birds.

At this cemetery you'll *know* for whom the bell tolls: Attendants will ring the 6-foot, 3,000-pound solid bronze Oishei bell cast in France upon request. Other highlights include the Blocher monument, with life-sized figures carved in Italian marble, and numerous unique monuments and mausoleums.

Sundays in June, July, and August, the staff offers two free tours. Several of the interred, such as President Fillmore, make guest appearances during the hour-long trolley tours that relate the cemetery's history. A forty-five-minute walking tour highlights the cemetery's natural attractions. The tours begin at 11:00 A.M. and conclude at 1:30 P.M. Call for exact times. (Tours are not given in inclement weather.)

Forest Lawn Cemetery & Garden Mausoleums, 1411 Delaware Avenue at Delavan, Buffalo 14209, (716) 885–1600, is open daily.

Mark Twain aficionados will want to visit the **Buffalo & Erie County Public Library**'s Rare Book Room. Among the thousands of manuscripts and first editions dating back to the fifteenth century is the original manuscript of *The Adventures of Huckleberry Finn*. The room also contains other mementos of Twain, a one-time Buffalo resident.

Buffalo and Erie County Public Library, Lafayette Square, Buffalo 14203, (716) 858–8900, is open October through April, Monday through Wednesday, Friday, and Saturday, 8:30 A.M. to 6:00 P.M.; Thursday, 8:30 A.M. to 8:00 P.M.; and Sunday, 1:00 to 5:00 P.M. Call for summer hours. Closed holidays.

Those buffalo-style chicken wings really were invented in Buffalo—at the **Anchor Bar and Restaurant,** which has been serving them up with celery and blue cheese dip since 1964. The restaurant has a reputation for good food, moderate prices, and large portions. It's at 1047 Main Street, (716) 886–8920.

Sample the city's other local specialty—beef on 'weck—at **Anderson's** or at **Charlie the Butcher;** both have several branches in the area.

More than 300 rare and unique bicycles and thousands of cycling-related collectibles span more than 175 years of bicycling history at the ◆**Pedaling History Bicycle Museum.**

Among the exhibits are a reproduction of the very first bicycle (made in 1817), an Irish Mail four-wheel velocipede, some "boneshakers" dating back to the 1860s, a pneumatic highwheel safety American Star, and an 1881 Marine bicycle. There are also extensive bicycle stein and lamp collections.

The Pedaling History Bicycle Museum, 3943 North Buffalo Road (Routes 277 & 240), Orchard Park 14127, (716) 662–3853, is open Monday through Saturday, 11:00 A.M. to 5:00 P.M.; Sunday, 1:30 to 5:00 P.M.; closed Tuesday, Wednesday, and Thursday, January 15 to April 1. Admission is $4.50 for adults, $4.00 for seniors, $2,50 for children ages 7 to 15, $12.50 for a family of up to four generations, and free to those over 80 years of age. Write or call for a listing of special free events.

LAKE ERIE SHORE

The southwestern tip of New York State is packed with as eclectic a mix of off-the-beaten-path sights as can be found anywhere. Remember kazoos—those funny little musical instruments you could play just by humming into them? They're still being made in Eden, at the **Original American Kazoo Company.** Established in 1916, it's now the only metal kazoo factory in the world—and it's still making them the same way they were made in 1916. The company used to produce everything from toy flutes and fishing tackle boxes to metal dog beds and peanut vending machines, but in 1965 the demand for kazoos became so great that the firm stopped manufacturing everything else.

The "working museum" at the Original American Kazoo Company shows how "America's only original musical instrument" is made, chronicles kazoo history, and regales visitors with such fascinating trivia as "'Far, Far Away' is the most requested tune played on the kazoo."

The Original American Kazoo Company, 8703 South Main Street, Eden 14057, (716) 992-3360, is open Monday through Saturday, 10:00 A.M. to 5:00 P.M.; Sunday, noon to 5:00 P.M. Closed Thanksgiving Day, Christmas Day, New Year's Day, Memorial Day, Easter, Fourth of July, and Labor Day. Admission is free.

Although it's now just a short hop off I-90, it's easy to imagine how isolated the **Dunkirk Historical Lighthouse** must have been when the lantern in the square, 61-foot tower first began guiding ships into Dunkirk Harbor in 1876. Today an automated light in the tower does the job, and the two-story, stick-style keeper's dwelling has been converted into a **Veteran's Park Museum.**

Five of the museum's rooms are devoted to displays of each branch of the military; five are preserved to show how the lighthouse keeper used to live; one is a memorial to the Vietnam era. An exhibit of maritime history and lake freighters is on display in the souvenir store. A separate building displays artifacts from the submarine service and Coast Guard.

Displays on the grounds include a 45-foot Lighthouse Buoy tender, a 21-foot rescue boat, and Civil War cannons. Visitors can take a tour of the lighthouse tower. An admission fee is charged for ground tours and tours of the museum.

Dunkirk Historical Lighthouse and Veteran's Park Museum, off Point Drive North, Dunkirk 14048, (716) 366–5050, are open April through June, 10:00 A.M. to 2:00 P.M. daily, except Sunday and Wednesday; July and August, 10:00 A.M. to 4:00 P.M. daily; and September through November, 10:00 A.M. to 3:00 P.M. daily, except Sunday and Wednesday.

Ready for a little beef on 'weck? Order "The Kaiser." Something fancier, like angel hair pasta with grilled chicken breast or tortellini Provençal? Stop at stately **White Inn** in Fredonia. Duncan Hines did, back in the 1930s, and was so taken with the food that he included it in his "Family of Fine Restaurants." Although the restaurant/inn has since undergone several transformations, it still proudly displays the Duncan Hines sign out front. And the building itself encompasses the original Victorian mansion built in 1868.

The White Inn, 52 East Main Street, Fredonia 14063, (716) 672–2103, is open daily year-round for lunch and dinner. Lunch is served Monday through

Saturday, 11:30 A.M. to 2:00 P.M.; dinner is served Monday through Thursday, 5:00 to 8:00 P.M., Friday and Saturday until 9:00 P.M., and Sunday, 12:30 until 8:00 P.M.

Antiquing and basket making have long been favorite activities in Chautauqua County, and ◆ **Stockton Sales** offers visitors a wealth of both. The building Dan and Carol Graziano bought in 1980 was originally known as the Stockton Basket Factory, and Carol still makes them today. She uses maple and cherry to craft a wide variety of shapes and designs, often adding stenciled designs. Many of her basket weaves and designs are original, and all are utilitarian as well as lovely.

And the merchandise at Stockton Sales? There are five buildings packed with antiques as well as one-of-a-kind items, memorabilia, and just plain old "stuff." At any given time a rough inventory might include oil paintings, carousel horses, animal mounts, barber poles, a Chinese cradle, a mounted water buffalo head, 1,000 chairs, 50 sets of china, . . . and on, and on, and on. The Grazianos also have a terrific selection of old books and encourage visitors to browse at their leisure.

Stockton Sales, 6 Mill Street, Stockton 14784, (716) 595-3516, is open June through August, Tuesday through Friday, 10:00 A.M. to 5:00 P.M., and Saturday, 1:00 to 5:00 P.M.; September through May, Tuesday through Friday, 10:00 A.M. to 4:00 P.M., and Saturday, 10:00 A.M. to 5:00 P.M. Closed Sunday and Monday.

Locals dubbed the sixteen-room mansion completed by James McClurg in 1820 "McClurg's Folly." He designed it, made and baked his own bricks, prepared local timber for the interior woodwork, and landscaped the spacious grounds with ornamental trees and shrubs and a water fountain stocked with goldfish.

Today the Chautauqua County Historical Society operates the restored frontier mansion as a museum and library and has filled it with furnishings, fine art, and local artifacts from its collection.

◆ **McClurg Museum,** Village Park, Routes 20 and 394, Westfield 14787, (716) 326-2977, is open Monday, Tuesday, and Thursday through Saturday from 1:00 to 5:00 P.M. Admission is $1.50 for adults, $1.00 for seniors, and 50 cents for children under 12.

At the northern tip of Chautauqua Lake in Mayville, the people at **Webb's Candy Factory** have been making goat's milk fudge for more than thirty years. The goats are gone from out back now and the milk comes from cans, but the confection is just as rich and creamy as ever, and the chocolate fudge with pecans is a regional taste treat not to be missed. Webb's makes all its candies by hand, using the old-fashioned, copper-kettle method, and has added a host of other treats to its repertoire, including "frogs," hard suckers, chocolate bars, divinity, and chocolate clusters. If you own a goat and want to start production, take a short tour of the candy factory between 10:00 A.M. and 4:00 P.M. Monday through Friday.

Webb's Candy Factory, Route 394, Mayville 14757, (716) 753-2161, is open daily, year-round. In summer the hours are 9:00 A.M. to 10:00 P.M.; in winter, 9:00 A.M. to 6:30 P.M.

Chautauqua Lake is also the home of a 122-year-old enterprise that exemplifies the American penchant for self-improvement. The ◈ **Chautauqua Institution** gave its name to an endless array of itinerant tent-show lyceums around the turn of the century. A lot of us have forgotten, though, that the original institution is still thriving right where it was founded in 1874. Chautauqua's progenitors were Bishop John Heyl Vincent and the industrialist (and father-in-law of Thomas Edison) Lewis Miller, and their original modest goal was the establishment of a school for Sunday-school teachers. Chautauqua grew to become a village unto itself, offering not only religious instruction but a program of lectures and adult-education courses.

The largely secularized Chautauqua of today bears little resemblance to the Methodist camp meeting of a hundred years ago, although services in the major faiths are held daily. The Chautauqua emphasis on culture and mental and spiritual improvement has led to an extensive annual summer calendar of lectures, classical and popular concerts, dramatic performances, and long- and short-term courses in subjects ranging from foreign languages to tap dancing to creative writing. It has its own 30,000-volume library.

To put it simply, Chautauqua is a vast summer camp of self-improvement, a place where you can rock (in chairs) on broad verandas, walk tree-lined streets that have no cars, and listen in on a chamber music rehearsal on your way to lunch.

The season at Chautauqua lasts for nine weeks each summer, but admission is available on a daily, weekend, or weekly basis.

For complete information on facilities and programs, contact Chautauqua Institution, 1 Ames

Street, Chautauqua 14722, (716) 357-6200 or (800) 836-ARTS.

Head south along the lake for a few miles to catch a ride on one of the last surviving modes of pioneer transport—the **Bemus Point–Stow Ferry.** The cable-drawn ferry has traversed the "narrows" of the lake at these points for more than 177 years. Unfortunately (or, for animal rights activists, fortunately), the oxen that once pulled the ferry with the aid of a treadmill and manila rope retired quite a while ago. But the pace and charm of the primitive open barge still remain.

The Bemus Point–Stow Ferry, Stow 14757 (mailing address: 15 Water Street, Mayville 14757), (716) 753-2403, is open from 11:00 A.M. to 9:00 P.M. Saturday and Sunday in June and daily in July and August. Admission is $3.00 per car and $1.00 per person for walk-ons.

Jamestown, birthplace of one of the country's leading naturalists, is home to his ◆ **Roger Tory Peterson Institute of Natural History,** housed in a handsome wood and stone building nestled on twenty-seven acres of woods and meadows.

The institute's mission is to train educators to help children discover the natural world around them. Part of this program involves changing exhibitions of wildlife art and nature photography at the institute, and the public is invited to visit, hike the surrounding trails, and visit the Butterfly Garden and gift shop.

The Roger Tory Peterson Institute of Natural History, 311 Curtis Street, Jamestown 14701, (716) 665-2473, is open Monday through Saturday, 10:00

A.M. to 4:00 P.M., and Sunday, 1:00 to 5:00 P.M. Admission fees vary depending on exhibits.

You found that stuffed water buffalo head you wanted back at Stockton Sales, but where to go to buy a turkey call or a genuine crock pickle? At ◆ **Lock, Stock & Barrel Country Store,** serving the people of Ellington since 1833. Lock, Stock & Barrel is the country store of our youth—jam-packed with penny candy, spices, candles, roasted peanuts, hunting and fishing equipment, and antiques and collectibles.

The rooms are as packed with history as they are with merchandise. The shelves in the main part of the store are original, as are the wooden floors and the kerosene lanterns hanging from the ceiling (now converted to electricity). Be sure to check the guest book before you leave: To date, visitors from all fifty states and fourteen countries have found their way to this off-the-beaten-path attraction.

Lock, Stock & Barrel Country Store, Town Square, Ellington 14732, (716) 287–3886, is open daily, except Tuesday, from 11:00 A.M. until 5:00 P.M. Memorial Day through Labor Day.

You'll notice a lot of goods made by the Amish at Lock, Stock & Barrel. That's because Ellington borders on **Amish Country,** which encompasses several towns to the north and east. The Amish first came to Cattaraugus County from Ohio in 1949. Although they prefer to live their own lifestyle, they're a friendly people who generally welcome questions about their way of life. (They do request, however, that you not take their picture.) There are a number of small shops on Route 62 in the town of **Conewango Valley** that offer products made by, or about, the Amish. **Franklin Graphics** sells Amish photos, books, and postcards. Stop at **Mueller's Valley View Cheese Factory** to sample Swiss cheese and forty other varieties made in Amish country. **Amish Country Fair** carries furniture and crafts.

ALLEGANY HEARTLAND

Salamanca is the only city in the world located on a Native American reservation; it is also home to the largest park in the state's park system. The **Seneca–Iroquois National Museum** on the Allegany Indian Reservation traces the cultural and historical heritage of the Seneca, known as "Keeper of the Western Door of the Iroquois Confederacy." The museum exhibits collections of artifacts beginning with prehistoric times and re-creates the culture and history of the Seneca people.

The Seneca-Iroquois National Museum, Broad Street Extension, Salamanca 14779, (716) 945-1738, is open April 1 through September 30, daily, 9:00 A.M. to 5:00 P.M.; October 1 through March 31, Monday through Friday, 9:00 A.M. to 5:00 P.M. Closed for the month of January and on Easter, American Indian Day, Thanksgiving Day, and Christmas Day. An entry fee is charged.

With 65,000 acres, two 100-acre lakes, and 80 miles of hiking trails, ◆ **Allegany State Park,** "the wilderness playground of western New York," is the largest of the state parks.

It's a mecca for both summer and winter outdoor enthusiasts. There are lakes for boating and swimming, ballfields, tennis courts, picnic areas, playgrounds, bike paths, and miles of cross-country and snowmobile trails. Rowboats and paddleboats can be rented at the Red House boathouse, where there are also a restaurant, tent and trailer area, and bicycle rental. The park has seasons for small game, turkey, archery deer, and big game. A special permit (free) is required to fish the park's waters.

Allegany State Park, off Route 17, Salamanca 14779, (716) 354-9101 or 354-9121, is open daily, year-round. There is no entrance fee.

Before you leave Salamanca, stop at the **Salamanca Rail Museum,** a fully restored passenger depot constructed in 1912 by the Buffalo, Rochester, and Pittsburgh Railroad. The museum uses exhibits, artifacts, and video presentations to re-create an era when rail was the primary means of transportation from city to city.

Salamanca Rail Museum, 170 Main Street, Salamanca 14779, (716) 945-3133, is open Monday through Saturday from 10:00 A.M. to 5:00 P.M. and Sunday from noon to 5:00 P.M. Closed the months of January, February, and March. Closed Monday in October, November, and December. Admission is free, but donations are welcomed.

Most of us have heard about how, in an effort to force Indians out west onto reservations in the late 1800s, the buffalo they relied on for food, clothing, and protection were slaughtered en masse. In 1850 twenty million buffalo roamed the western plains. By 1900 only a couple of hundred could be found.

But research now shows that buffalo meat is lower in cholesterol than fish or chicken and has 25 percent more protein than beef. America's "original meat" is becoming *the* choice of health-conscious Americans, and buffalo are once again roaming the fruited plains (plums go particularly well with bison) in increasing numbers.

So when Glenn and Lorri Bayger decided to start a ranch and considered raising beef cattle, they were advised by experts to invest in buffalo instead. Today a herd of 300 roam over 610 open acres at the ◆ **B & B Buffalo Ranch** in Ellicottville. Visitors are invited to learn about buffalo and visit the store, which sells souvenirs, Indian jewelry, and, of course, buffalo meat.

The store at the B & B Buffalo Ranch, Horn Hill Road, Ellicottville 14731, (716) 699-8813, is open from May 1 through December 31, Tuesday through Saturday, 10:00 A.M. to 5:00 P.M., and Sunday, 11:00 A.M. to 5:00 P.M.; from January 1 through April 30, Thursday through Saturday, 10:00 A.M. to 5:00 P.M., and Sunday, 1:00 to 5:00 P.M.

Head north on Route 219 a short distance to Ashford Hollow to see one of the most unconventional sculpture "gardens" ever. For more than thirty years, local sculptor Larry Griffis has been integrating his art with nature—placing his monumental abstract/representational creations throughout a 400-acre woodland setting/nature preserve. More than 200 of his pieces, most made of steel and between 20 and 30 feet high, are on exhibit at **Griffis Sculpture Park.** Ten nudes ring a pond, sharing the banks with live swans and ducks. A towering mosquito awaits unwary hikers along one of the 10 miles

Griffis Sculpture Park

of hiking trails. Giant toadstools grow in a field, waiting to be climbed on.

Griffis Sculpture Park, Route 219, Ahrens Road, Ashford Hollow (mailing address: 6902 Valley Road, East Otto 14729), (716) 257-9344, is open daily, May through October from 9:00 A.M. to 9:00 P.M. Closed November through April. Admission is free. Tours are given by appointment.

About 320 million years ago, river and delta sediments were deposited on the eroded surface of Devonian shoals. Crystalline igneous and metamorphic rocks with milky quartz veins were exposed and long transportation of the sediments selectively weathered and eroded the nonquartz minerals.

What all this means is that ◆ **Rock City** is one of the world's largest exposures of quartz conglomerate (pudding stone), a place where you can wander through crevices and past towering, colorfully named formations like Fat Man's Squeeze, Tepee Rock, and Signal Rock, with its 1,000-square-mile view.

Rock City, Route 16A, Olean 14760, (716) 372–7790, is open daily from May 1 through October (except in bad weather). Admission is $4.00 for adults, $3.50 for senior citizens, and $2.00 for children 6 to 12.

If you were heading off to a summer at Chautauqua three generations ago, you would have gotten there by rail—specifically by a steam-hauled train of the Erie, Pennsylvania, or New York Central railroads. Of course, Amtrak can get you there today (nearest station: Erie, Pennsylvania), but if you want steam, you'll have to head to a nostalgia operation like the ◆ **Arcade and Attica Railroad,** headquartered just southeast of Buffalo in Arcade.

Maybe *nostalgia* isn't the right word, since the Arcade and Attica is a real working railroad with a healthy freight clientele. But the company's passenger operation is an unabashed throwback, relying for motive power on a pair of circa 1920 coal burners pulling old, open-window steel coaches that once belonged to the Delaware, Lackawanna, and Western. Arcade and Attica passengers enjoy a ninety-minute ride through some of upstate's loveliest farm country, ending right where they started by way of a trip back through time.

The Arcade and Attica Railroad, 278 Main Street, Arcade 14009, (716) 496-9877, operates weekends from Memorial Day through the end of October, with Wednesday and Friday trips during July and August. Call ahead for schedules. Tickets are available at the 278 Main Street office.

Horse lovers can roll out of bed and onto a mount for a trail ride through the Colden Hills at ◆ **Pipe Creek Farm B & B,** a working equine farm. The three-bedroom inn has shared baths and an in-ground pool. Rates range from $50 to $70 and include a full country breakfast. In addition to trail rides, owners Phil and Kathy Crone give lessons in hunt seat, stock seat, and saddle seat. In the winter there are 200 acres of cross-country ski trails to enjoy.

Pipe Creek Farm B & B, Falls Road, West Falls 14170, (716) 652-4868, is open all year.

One of the most interesting personalities of turn-of-the-century America was a self-made philosopher named Elbert Hubbard. In addition to writing a little "preachment" (as he called it) titled "A Message to Garcia" that dealt with the themes of loyalty and hard work, and publishing his views in a periodical called the *Philistine,* Hubbard was famous for having imported the design aesthetic and celebration of handcrafts fostered in England by the artist and poet William Morris. Elbert Hubbard became the chief American proponent of the Arts and Crafts movement, which touted the virtues of honest craftsmanship in the face of an increasing tendency in the late nineteenth century toward machine production of furniture, printed matter, and decorative and utilitarian household objects.

Visually, the style absorbed influences as diverse as art nouveau and American Indian crafts and is familiar to most of us in the form of solid, oaken, slat-sided Morris chairs and the simple "Mission" furniture of Gustav Stickley. Elbert Hubbard not only wrote about such stuff but also set up a community of craftspeople to turn it out—furniture, copper, leather, even printed books. He called his operation The Roycrofters, and it was headquartered on a "Campus" in East Aurora.

There are several ways the modern traveler can savor the spirit of Elbert Hubbard in modern East Aurora. One is by visiting the **Roycroft Campus,** on South Grove Street. The campus grounds, now a National Historic Site, feature a gift shop, working pottery, art gallery, and several antiques dealers, all housed in Hubbard-era buildings. For information contact the East Aurora Chamber of Commerce, 666 Main Street, East Aurora 14052, (716) 652–8444.

Another window on the Roycroft era is the **Elbert Hubbard-Roycroft Museum,** recently located in a 1910 bungalow built by Roycroft craftsmen and now on the National Register of Historic Places. Part of the furnishings, including the superb Arts & Crafts Dining Room, are original and were the property of centenarian Grace ScheideMantel when she turned the house over to the museum in 1985. (Mrs. Scheide-Mantel's husband, George, once headed the Roycroft leather department.) Other Roycroft products on display at the house include a magnificent stained-glass lamp by Roycroft designer Dard Hunter and a saddle custom-made for Hubbard just prior to his death on the torpedoed *Lusitania* in 1915.

There is a wonderful period garden, complete with a sundial and a "gazing ball," maintained by "The Masters Gardeners" of the Erie County Cooperative Extension Service.

The Elbert Hubbard Museum (ScheideMantel House), 363 Oakwood Avenue, East Aurora 14052, (716) 652-4735, is open from June 1 to mid-October on Wednesday, Saturday, and Sunday, 2:00 to 4:00 P.M.; by appointment the rest of the year. A $1.00 donation is requested. Private or group tours also can be arranged, year-round, by appointment.

Elbert Hubbard opened ◆ **The Roycroft Inn** in 1903 to accommodate the people who came to visit his Roycroft community of craftsmen. When he died, his son took over management. In 1986 the inn was granted National Landmark Status and, after extensive renovations, reopened in 1995. It's furnished with Arts & Crafts pieces, many of them original, and the floor plan and style are in keeping with the inn's original fabric.

The Roycroft Inn, 40 South Grove Street, East Aurora 14052, (716) 652-5552, is open year-round. Call for rates.

◆ **Toy Town Museum** is a must for anybody traveling with kids. The museum/children's activity center displays a large collection of antique toys (including many by local manufacturer Fisher-Price), as well as Toyworks for lots of "hands-on" fun. The museum hosts its annual three-day Toyfest each August.

Toy Town Museum, 606 Girard Avenue, East Aurora 14052, (716) 687-5151, is open Monday through Saturday, 10:00 A.M. to 4:00 P.M. There is an admission fee.

Before taking leave of East Aurora, we should stop in at the home of one of our least appreciated presidents, Millard Fillmore. Fillmore, who was born in the Finger Lakes town of Genoa in 1800, came to East Aurora to work as a lawyer in 1825. He built this house (since moved to its present Shearer Avenue location) on Main Street, in the village, in the same year and lived here with his wife until 1830. As restored and furnished by previous owners and the Aurora Historical Society, the **Millard Fillmore House National Landmark** contains country furnishings of Fillmore's era, as well as more refined pieces in the Greek Revival, or "Empire," style of the president's early years. A high desk to be used while standing was part of the furnishings in Fillmore's law office; the rear parlor, added in 1930, showcases furniture owned by the Fillmores in later years, when they lived in a Buffalo mansion. The large bookcase was used in the White House during the Fillmore presidency.

The Millard Fillmore House National Landmark (Aurora Historical Society), 24 Shearer Avenue, East Aurora 14052, (716) 652-8875, is open from June 1 to mid-October, Wednesday, Saturday, and Sunday, 2:00 to 4:00 P.M.; by appointment the rest of the year. A donation of $2.00 is requested.

The village of ◆ **Wyoming,** settled in the early 1800s, is gaslit and has more than seventy buildings on the Historic Register. It's filled with charming shops such as the **Gaslight Christmas Shoppe, Silas Newell's Provisions,** and **Krammel's Meat Market,** purveyors of delicious homemade sausages. Stop for a cappuccino at the **Gaslight Village Cafe and Pub** or tea, homemade treats, and the night at the circa 1825 **Wyoming Inn B & B** (716-495-6470).

If you want to stay a bit out of town, **Hillside Inn,** on forty-eight acres of woods, streams, hills, and ravines, has twelve guest rooms. Built in 1851 as a health spa, the classic Greek Revival mansion serves an innovative American cuisine featuring entrees such as charred yellowfin tuna and sautéed tournadoes of beef in a cabernet and black pepper sauce. Rates, which include a continental breakfast, begin at $60 in winter for a room in Hollyhock Cottage, and at $90 for a room in the mansion. Hillside Inn is located at 890 East Bethany Road, Wyoming 14591, (716)495-6800 or (800) 544-2249.

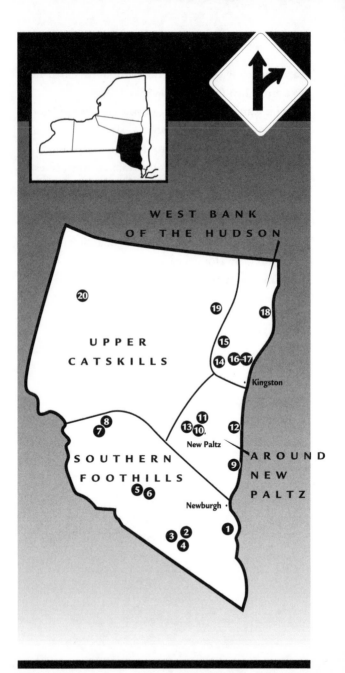

WEST BANK
OF THE HUDSON

20

19   18

UPPER
CATSKILLS

15
14   16-17

· Kingston

11
13 10.   12

New Paltz

SOUTHERN
FOOTHILLS   AROUND

9   NEW

5 6

PALTZ

Newburgh ·

3 2   1
4

7 8

THE CATSKILLS

1. Constitution Island
2. Brotherhood (winery)
3. Harness Racing Museum and Hall of Fame
4. Sugar Loaf Arts and Craft Village
5. Inn at Lake Joseph
6. Wurtsboro Airport
7. Apple Pond Farming Center
8. Catskill Fly Fishing Center and Museum
9. Gomez Mill House
10. Huguenot Street
11. Delaware and Hudson Canal Museum
12. Slabsides
13. Mohonk Mountain House
14. Onteora, The Mountain House
15. Kaatskill Kaleidoscope
16. Opus 40
17. Saugerties Lighthouse
18. Bronck Museum
19. Richter's Butterfly Museum
20. Hanford Mills Museum

THE CATSKILLS

To many lifelong New York City residents for whom the Adirondacks might as well be the other side of the moon, the Catskills *are* upstate New York. At this point in our travels, we certainly know better—but nevertheless, if you had only a couple of days to get out of the city, the Catskills would be your best bet for a quick introduction to exurban New York.

The Catskills, of course, are "mountains" in the eastern rather than the western sense. Generally lower in elevation than the Adirondacks, these are old, worn peaks, part of the Appalachian Range. The higher elevations are to the north, where the larger ski areas are located. But some of the most dramatic Catskills scenery lies along the west shore of the Hudson, within 30 or 40 miles of the New York City line. Here are the majestic Palisades, brooding cliffs of volcanic basalt exposed by millions of years of water and weather; here also are Bear Mountain, Tallman, and Harriman state parks, with their thick forests and panoramic views. Farther west are the abrupt cliffs of the Shawangunk Mountains, where some of the world's greatest rock climbers perfect their technique.

A place of mystery to the early Dutch settlers, and later a virtual synonym for a certain style of resort entertainment, the Catskill region has a history as varied as its terrain. We'll start our exploration at the south, near the Hudson, and move north and then west toward the farther hills.

SOUTHERN FOOTHILLS

Just about everyone knows where West Point is, but how many Hudson Valley travelers or military buffs can locate ◆ **Constitution Island**? Geographic literalists might look for it in the first chapter of this book, since it's practically on the east shore of the Hudson, separated from the mainland only by marshes. But since visitors have to take a boat to get to the island, and since the boat leaves from West Point, we have it here among our Catskill sites.

Although Constitution Island never served any military purpose after the Revolutionary War, it had an important part to play in General Washington's strategy for keeping British naval traffic out of the upper Hudson River. During the earlier part of the war, the fortifications on the island were relatively ineffectual; begun in 1775, **Fort Constitution** was still unfinished when it was captured by the British two years later. Largely destroyed by its American defenders before they retreated, the fort was never rebuilt.

By the following year, however, the island was back in American hands and was more valuable than ever in view of its position opposite the new American defenses constructed at West Point. Here was a place where British ships could be stopped dead in the water, and the way to do it was to stretch an immense iron chain across the river from West Point to Constitution Island. The chain was forged of stout New Jersey iron (a portion of it can be seen at the state reservation at Ringwood, New Jersey), floated across the river on rafts of logs, and securely anchored at either shore. Three redoubts and a battery were constructed on Constitution Island to protect the eastern end of the chain.

The chain did its job, and Constitution Island saw no further hostilities throughout the remaining five years of the war.

Constitution gained fame in the nineteenth century as the home of the Warner sisters, Susan (1819–85) and Anna (1824–1915). Under pseudonyms the two sisters wrote a total of 106 books, collaborating on 18 of them. Part of the present-day tour of the island is a visit to the **Warner House,** fifteen rooms of which are furnished in the Victorian style of the Warner sisters' heyday.

Constitution Island is open to guided two-hour tours from mid-June through the end of September. Boats leave West Point South Dock at 1:00 and 2:00 P.M. Wednesday and Thursday afternoons. Fare and admission to the house and fort are $8.00 for adults, $7.00 for senior citizens and students, and $2.00 for children under 5. For information contact the Constitution Island Association, Box 41, West Point 10996, (914) 446–8676. Reservations are recommended.

In the 1830s John Jaques emigrated from Europe to the small town of Washingtonville. Trained as a shoe- and bootmaker, he planned to support himself with his trade. To augment his income he purchased ten acres of land on Main Street and planted grapes in the rich, loamy Hudson Valley soil to sell at market. When he became a church elder, he used some of his grapes to make sacramental wine.

Today ◈ **Brotherhood** is America's oldest winery, and the church where Mr. Jaques's wine was first served is the winery's gift shop. Brotherhood has been making wine continuously since 1839, having survived Prohibition by once again reverting to the sale of sacramental wine. Its vast underground cellars, comparable to those of famous European wineries, are the largest in the country, and, in addition to sacramental wine, Brotherhood now makes specialty, table, dessert, and premium vintage wines—including Grand Monarque champagne.

A tour of the winery includes a visit to the underground cellars and a sampling of a half-dozen wines.

Brotherhood, 35 North Street, Washingtonville 10992, (914) 496–9101, offers guided wine-tasting tours daily from May through October and on weekend afternoons from November through April. Admission is $4.00 for adults, $2.00 for children ages 15 to 20, and free for children under 15. Call for a calendar of weekend events.

Orange County is known for its fine standardbred horses—the horses of the harness track. Hambletonian, sire of virtually all of today's trotters, was born here. For years it has been home to the Trotting Horse Museum, Home of the Hall of Fame of the Trotter. The museum has officially changed its name to the ◈ **Harness Racing Museum & Hall of Fame** and is planning to reopen in July 1997 after extensive renovations. Included among the changes is interactive technology including the first 3-D simulator designed for the horse-racing industry, which will let visitors feel what it's like to drive a horse in an actual race.

Harness Racing Museum & Hall of Fame

The Harness Racing Museum & Hall of Fame, 240 Main Street, Goshen 10924, (914) 294-6330. Call for information on hours and admission fees.

Across the way is **Goshen Historic Track,** the oldest active harness track in the country and the first sporting site in the nation to be designated a National Registered Historic Landmark by the National Park Service.

Many of the region's fine artists and craftspeople have studios and/or galleries in ◆ **Sugar Loaf Arts and Craft Village,** a complex of more than eighty-five shops, galleries, and restaurants. More than forty crafters display their works at **Partners in Crafts.**

Potters Ray and Terry Boswell make stoneware, porcelain, raku, and terra-cotta pieces at **Bostree Pottery and Jewelry. Cheshire Glass Gallery** displays works of sixty American glass blowers. The village is a browser's paradise.

Sugar Loaf Arts and Craft Village, Kings Highway, Sugar Loaf 10981, (914) 469–9181, is open Tuesday through Sunday, 11:00 A.M. to 5:00 P.M. There are special events throughout the year. Call for a list.

The next time you eat an onion, consider this: It might well have been grown in black dirt formed 12,000 years ago in a glacial lake in an area now known as **Pine Island.** As the glaciers melted and the climate warmed, vegetation grew, died, and sank to the bottom of the lake. The lake area earned the nickname "the drowned lands" and remained a swamp until the early 1900s, when immigrants came, bought the land cheap, drained the lake by hand, built drainage ditches, and then planted onions in the rich black dirt. Today, with thousands of acres planted, the "black dirt" region is one of the country's leading producers of onions.

The cream of onion soup at **Ye Jolly Onion Inn** is made from Pine Island onions. So are the deep-fried onion blossoms, the onion rings, and the onion gravy on the Pine Island steak. And the vegetables on the salad bar are all from farms in the area (in season). After a visit to the "black dirt" region and Ye Jolly Onion Inn, you'll never again think lightly of the humble onion.

Ye Jolly Onion Inn, corner of Route 517, Pulaski Highway and Orange County Route 1, Pine Island

10969, (914) 258-4277, is open Wednesday and Thursday, 5:00 to 9:00 P.M.; Friday and Saturday, 5:00 to 10:00 P.M.; and Sunday, noon to 7:30 P.M.

If your interest in horses has been piqued by the Harness Racing Museum & Hall of Fame, head over to **New Hope Farms** in Port Jervis. With eighty acres it's one of the largest equestrian facilities in the nation and features indoor and outdoor arenas and permanent stabling for 100 horses. Visitors are invited to stop by at any time to watch thoroughbreds and warmbloods being trained for show jumping competitions.

The first weekend in May, New Hope Farms hosts the Royal Dressage Festival (there's a gate charge), and the week after Labor Day, the Autumn Classic (free except for a charge for the Grand Prix Saturday night). And throughout the year there are events such as a tri-state rodeo, a family festival, and a championship dressage. The indoor arena, which seats 3,000, is the largest in the country.

New Hope Farms, 500 Neversink Drive, Port Jervis 12771, (914) 856-8384 or 856-4007, is open daily, year-round, from 8:00 A.M. to 5:00 P.M. From the end of January through March 15, most of the horses are moved south and there's very little activity.

The ◆ **Inn at Lake Joseph** is a Victorian country estate high in the Catskill Mountains. It nestles against a 250-acre lake and is surrounded by thousands of acres of forest and wildlife preserve.

Built by Thomas Hunt Talmadge in the latter part of the nineteenth century, the estate served as a retreat for the Dominican Sisters, as a vacation home of Cardinals

Hayes and Spellman of New York, and finally as a scrumptious inn.

Several of the inn's ten guest rooms in the main house have working fireplaces and whirlpool baths. If you yearn for even more privacy, request a room in the recently restored turn-of-the-century Adirondack-style carriage house. "The Cottage," in a secluded corner of the carriage house, is the most private guest room in the inn. Meals are served, and there are plenty of outdoor sporting activities—including paddling around in a Victorian-style swimming pool. Lake Joseph has a reputation as one of the finest largemouth bass lakes in the state.

Inn at Lake Joseph, 400 St. Joseph Road, Forestburgh 12777, (914) 791-9506, is open year-round. Call for rates.

From December through March (eagle time) Sullivan County becomes home to a large concentration of migrant **bald eagles**—mostly from Canada. A few of their favorite nesting places include Mongaup Falls Reservoir and Rio Reservoir in Forestburgh and the Rondout Reservoir in Grahamsville. For an update and complete list of sites contact The Audubon Society of New York State, P.O. Box 111, Eldred 12732, (914) 557-8025.

Getting from one place to another quickly and with panache is an American preoccupation. In the nineteenth century a fast trotting horse might have done the trick; in the twentieth we have the option of zipping along on or off the ground. If you like the idea of slipping silently through the air and didn't get your chance at the National Soaring Museum in Elmira (see The

Finger Lakes chapter), you'll find another opportunity in the southern Catskills at ◆ **Wurtsboro Airport.**

Established in 1927, Wurtsboro bills itself as the oldest soaring site in the nation. The airport's Flight Service is the largest soaring school in the United States, offering lessons for people with no flight experience as well as for those licensed to fly power planes. For the casual visitor, however, the big attraction is the demonstration rides. After being towed aloft by a single-engine Cessna, you'll glide high above the Catskills with an FAA-rated commercial pilot at the stick. The demonstration ride lasts fifteen to twenty minutes and costs $32.00. For $5.00 more you can turn your joyride into an introductory lesson.

Wurtsboro Airport and Flight Service, Route 209, Wurtsboro 12790, (914) 888-2791, is open daily, all year, 9:00 A.M. to 6:00 P.M. or dusk, whichever comes first. Closed major holidays.

You've got to love a place that advertises "Children & Pets Very Welcome." ◆ **Apple Pond Farming Center**—a working farm, educational center, and B & B perched on a ridge in the Catskills—offers a totally different vacation experience. The emphasis here is on "working"; the owners farm with horses and have twenty-five of them to help out. They breed American Paint, Pinto Sporting, and Belgian Draft horses, and they have 100 sheep and goats and several Scottish Border Collies.

Visitors can help with a variety of chores if they wish, or opt for workshops on horses, wool spinning, organic gardening, or trail rides; or they can just kick back, relax, and canoe or swim in the nearby Delaware River.

Apple Pond Farming Center, Box 65, Hahn Road, Callicoon Center 12724, (914) 482–4764, is open year-round. Amenities in the three-bedroom guest house include a large Jacuzzi, sunroom, kitchen, bath, and several decks. Rates range from $65 a night in the B & B to $500 a week for the guest house, which is large enough to accommodate two families.

According to the folks at **Memories,** buyers searched five states and three countries to fill their 20,000-square-foot-building with more than 25,000 unique items covering every style and taste from the early 1800s to the 1950s. Furniture, lamps, clocks, rocking horses, decoys, glass, china, magazines, and, as they say, "who knows what's coming in?"

Memories, Route 17 Quickway, Parksville 12768, (914) 292–4270 or (800) ABC–TIME, is open daily, year-round, 10:00 A.M. to 5:00 P.M.

Many devotees of fly-fishing believe that, in North America, the sport began in the Catskills. And seeing the streams that run along the Beaverkill and Willowemoc valleys, it's hard to imagine a more suitable birthplace—or a more suitable location for a center devoted to preserving the heritage and protecting the future of fly-fishing in the United States. That's the mission of the ◆ **Catskill Fly Fishing Center and Museum,** on the shores of the Willowemoc River between Roscoe and Livingston Manor.

Founded in 1891, the new facility, which opened in May 1995, illuminates the contributions and lives of the great names associated with the Catskill era—Gordon and Hewitt, Dette and Darbee, LaBranche and Flick—as well as Lee Wulff, Poul

Jorgensen, and other from the world of fly-fishing. Interpretive exhibits on the evolution of the sport, as well as hundreds of meticulously crafted rods, flies, and reels are on display. Special guest fly tyers demonstrate their craft every Saturday afternoon throughout the season. The center offers a variety of educational and recreational programs year-round, including courses in stream ecology and angling, fly tying, and rod building.

Catskill Fly Fishing Center and Museum, (mailing address: P. O. Box 1295, Livingston Manor 12758), (914) 439–4810, is open daily, 10:00 A.M. to 4:00 P.M. from mid-March through October; weekdays, 10:00 A.M. to 4:00 P.M. the rest of the year. Closed holidays.

In the 1970s Al Zuckerman of Grahamsville learned that he is a direct descendant of Kalonymus, a Sicilian Jew who rescued Otto II, the Holy Roman emperor, from drowning after he was thrown from his horse—in full armor—into the surf in A.D. 982. A cliff on Mr. Zucherman's property is now a U.S. historical landmark dedicated to the young savior's memory. A museum adjacent to the memorial exhibits relics relating to Kalonymus and local memorabilia of Sullivan County.

Kalonymus Escarpment, Five Dave Road, Grahamsville 12740, (914) 985–2497, is open free, year-round, 10:00 A.M. to 4:00 P.M. by appointment only.

AROUND NEW PALTZ

In 1714 Louis Moses Gomez, a refugee from the Spanish Inquisition, purchased 6,000 acres of land along the Hudson highlands and built a fieldstone blockhouse. Today, the ◆ **Gomez Mill House** is the earliest surviving Jewish residence in North America.

Over the ensuing years the house was purchased by others, who made changes to the original structure. The most famous twentieth-century owner was the Craftsman-era designer Dard Hunter, who rebuilt the old gristmill on "Jew's Creek" into a paper mill and then made paper by hand, cut and cast type, and handprinted his own books.

Today the house, continuously inhabited for more than 280 years, is being restored and preserved by the Gomez Foundation for Mill House; the foundation is made up of friends and descendants of families who lived here.

The Gomez Mill House, Mill House Road, Marlboro 12542, (914) 236–3126, is open mid-April through October, Wednesday, Saturday, and Sunday from 10:00 A.M. to 4:00 P.M. and Thursday and Friday by appointment.

The gristmill at **Tuthilltown Gristmill & Country Store** has been grinding flour and meal without interruption since 1788! The historic landmark was grinding while Napoleon fought in Austria . . . grinding through the War of 1812 . . . grinding when Abraham Lincoln and John F. Kennedy were shot . . . grinding when this book went to press. . . .

Little has changed over the years, but a store at the rear of the building now sells stone-ground flours and grains, pancake and waffle mixes, and a host of other baking ingredients and gift items.

Tuthilltown Gristmill & Country Store, 1020 Albany Post Road, Gardiner 12525, (914) 255–5695, is

Tuthilltown Grist Mill & Country Store

open June until Christmas, Wednesday through Sunday; mid-January through May, Thursday through Sunday; closed Christmas to mid-January. There is an admission fee to enter the mill.

Back in the old Hudson Valley town of New Paltz, we encounter one of those odd superlatives—something you might never have devoted a moment's curiosity to but is nonetheless fascinating once discovered. This is ◆ **Huguenot Street,** the oldest street in America that still has its original houses. Think about it: Find a street where each building lot has had only one house upon it, and chances are you're in a 1950s subdivision. But the stone houses on Huguenot Street were built between 1692 and 1712, and they'll look good for at least another 300 years.

Persecuted by the Catholic majority in their native France and displaced by the incessant religious warfare of the seventeenth century, many Huguenots—peaceful members of a Protestant sect—came to southern New York in pursuit of freedom and tolerance. In 1677 twelve of their number purchased the lands around present-day New Paltz from the Esopus Indians and built log huts as their first habitations.

As the twelve pioneers and their families prospered, they decided to build more permanent dwellings. And permanent they were. Here are five perfectly preserved houses, with additions that were built on by the settlers' descendants over the years. All of the houses are maintained by the Huguenot Historical Society, which gives tours Wednesday through Sunday from Memorial Day weekend through September. Tours are available at varying rates and durations. For information contact the Huguenot Society, P.O. Box 339, New Paltz 12561, (914) 255-1660 or 255-1889.

Just north of New Paltz, at High Falls, is a museum dedicated to a great work of engineering brought about because of an energy crisis. No, this one had nothing to do with OPEC or Iranian crude—it was the crisis in coal supply brought about by America's 1812-14 war with Great Britain. Two Wurts brothers, Maurice and William, figured that a canal was the way to bring Pennsylvania anthracite (hard coal) from the mines to New York City and vicinity, thus avoiding future shortages brought about by depending on foreign suppliers.

The two men formed the Delaware and Hudson Canal Company in 1825, with the stated purpose of linking Honesdale, Pennsylvania, with the Hudson River port of Eddyville, New York. The surveying and engineering of the 108-mile route was handled by Benjamin Wright, chief engineer of the Erie Canal. The Delaware and Hudson Canal, completed in 1828, was the first million-dollar enterprise in America. Between 1847 and 1852 it was enlarged and deepened to accommodate heavier traffic. A lot of coal came down in barges along the old route, but the company that built it made a bold move in 1829 that would soon doom canals and the way of life they represented. In that year the company began to work its gravity-operated rail line between Honesdale and Carbondale, Pennsylvania, with a new English contraption called a steam locomotive. Except for a few weedy stretches, the canal is gone—but the Delaware and Hudson Railroad survives to this day as the oldest transportation company in the United States.

The ◆ **Delaware and Hudson Canal Museum** is a private institution established to tell the story of the old canal, and it does so not merely through glassed-in exhibits but by preserving the extant structures, channel, and locks in the High Falls vicinity. Visitors learn about the canal through sophisticated dioramas, photos, and technological exhibits, including models of a working lock and gravity railroad. There are five locks at High Falls. The Delaware and Hudson Canal Historical Society has done whatever restoration and preservation work is possible on them and has linked canal sites in the area with a system of hiking trails. Self-guided tours take in nearby canal segments as well as the remains of John Roebling's suspension aqueduct.

The Delaware and Hudson Canal Museum, Mohonk Road, High Falls 12440, (914) 687-9311, is open Memorial Day weekend through Labor Day, Thursday, Friday, Saturday, and Monday, 11:00 A.M. to 5:00 P.M. and Sunday 1:00 to 5:00 P.M. Also open weekends in May, September, and October, Saturday, 11:00 A.M. to 5:00 P.M., and Sunday, 1:00 to 5:00 P.M. A suggested donation is $2.00 for adults, $1.00 for children, and $5.00 for families. Members are free.

The prodigious industrial expansion made possible by canals and railroads in the America of the nineteenth century was often accomplished at the expense of the natural environment, a phenomenon that persists in our own day. Fortunately the 1800s also produced great pioneers of the conservationist spirit, whose writings and example point the way for those who continue their struggle today. Among them, of course, are the Californian John Muir and his equally dedicated, near-contemporary John Burroughs, a native New Yorker who wrote twenty-five books on natural history and the philosophy of conservation. In 1895 Burroughs built a rustic log hideaway in the woods outside the village of West Park, barely 2 miles from the west bank of the Hudson. He called it ◆ **Slabsides,** and it is a National Historic Landmark today.

Burroughs, whose permanent home was only a mile and a half away, came to his little retreat to write and to quietly observe his natural surroundings. John Muir came here to talk with Burroughs, as did Theodore Roosevelt and Thomas Edison. They sat around the fire on log furniture of Burroughs's own manufacture, much of it still in the cabin.

Slabsides, which was deeded to the John Burroughs Association after the author's death in 1921, now stands within the 191-acre **John Burroughs Sanctuary,** a pleasant woodland tract that forms a most fitting living monument to his memory. The sanctuary is open all year; on the third Saturday in May and the first Saturday in October, the John Burroughs Association holds an open house from noon to 4:00 P.M. In addition to an opportunity to see the cabin, the special days include informal talks and nature walks. Admission is free. For further information write the association at 15 West Seventy-seventh Street, New York City 10024, or call (914) 384–6320 or (212) 769–5169.

Nestled in the heart of a 24,000-acre natural area in the Shawangunk Mountains, overlooking Lake Mohonk, is a sprawling Victorian castle-resort called the ◆**Mohonk Mountain House.** And above the Mohonk Mountain House stands **Sky Top Tower,** an observation tower built in 1923 of Shawangunk conglomerate that was quarried at its base. From the top of Sky Top Tower, on a clear day, you can see forever— or at least as far as the Rondout and Wallkill valleys, New Jersey, Connecticut, Vermont, Pennsylvania, and Massachusetts. The tower is also known as the Albert K. Smiley Memorial Tower in tribute to the founder of the Mohonk Mountain House, and even if you're not an overnight guest you can pay a day-visitor fee that will give you access to the tower; the many miles of hiking trails, paths, and carriage roads; and the lovely landscaped grounds.

Day visitors are also invited to visit the **Barn Museum,** in one of the largest barns in the Northeast.

Built in 1888, it houses more than fifty nineteenth-century horse-drawn vehicles and many working tools made more than one hundred years ago. The Barn Museum, (914) 255-1000, ext. 2447, is open Wednesday, Saturday, and Sunday. In the winter day visitors can cross-country ski on more than 35 miles of marked, maintained cross-country ski trails. In the summer and fall a shuttle ($2.00 per person round-trip) runs to and from Picnic Lodge—the day-visitor center—and the parking lot.

The Mohonk Mountain House, Lake Mohonk, New Paltz 12561, (914) 255-1000. Day-visitor pass cost is $6.00 for adults midweek and $9.00 weekends and holidays; $4.00 for children under 12 midweek and $5 weekends and holidays; and, for families with children under 12, $16.00 midweek and $23.00 weekends and holidays.

In 1928 the Rennie family of Ulster Park built a home from a Gordon-Van Tine kit. Today **Rennie's** is a beautifully restored B & B with classic Mission-style furnishings and works of local artists and craftspeople on display. There are four guest rooms ranging in price from $75 to $95. The B & B, 25 Ulster Avenue, Ulster Park 12487, (914) 331-5560 or (800) 447-8262, is open year-round.

WEST BANK OF THE HUDSON

When mayonnaise king Richard Hellmann was told, at the age of fifty-five, that he only had six months to live unless he moved to the country, he did what any sane millionaire would do. (No he didn't go to the Mayo Clinic.) He built a magnificent estate on the side of

Mount Ticetonyk overlooking the Esopus River valley, moved there with his family, and lived to be ninety-four.

Now a B & B, ◆ **Onteora, The Mountain House** (Onteora is the Mohican name for the Catskills, which translates to "the land and the sky") is surrounded by 225 acres of forest and features a magnificent multi-windowed 20- by 30-foot Great Room with a massive stone fireplace; a 40-foot covered dining porch with Adirondack-style tree trunk columns and railings; and a new 60-foot southwest deck. One of the five guest rooms has a private bath. The house is filled with an eclectic collection of antiques and Japanese and Korean art.

Onteora, The Mountain House, Piney Point Road, Boiceville 12412, (914) 657–6233, is open year-round. Rates, which include a full breakfast (with items such as crepes with three fillings and Eggs Hellmann), range from $85 a weekday night for a double with shared bath to $230 a weekend night for a combination room—two rooms for two with a connecting sun-room, gas fireplace, and shared bath.

Floating down Esopus Creek on a lazy afternoon as it winds through the Catskill Mountains is the ulti-mate vacation: relaxing, scenic, and fun. **The Town Tinker** rents tubes, helps chart your course, provides instruction as needed, and arranges transportation. There are separate 2½-mile routes for beginner and expert tubers. Transportation is provided by either Town Tinker Tube Taxis and/or the Catskill Mountain Railroad (see below).

The Town Tinker, Bridge Street (Route 28), Phoenicia 12464, (914) 688–5553, is open daily May through September from 9:00 A.M. to 6:00 P.M. Basic inner tubes rent for $7.00 a day. There is an additional charge for other equipment. Note: Novice tubers rent equipment at a substation at Mt. Pleasant Lodge, Catskill Corners, on Route 28 between Kingston and Phoenicia. Call ahead to verify which location you should go to.

On weekends and holidays **Catskill Mountain Railroad** transports novice tubers back to Phoenicia at the end of their run (one-way fare is $4.00). But if you'd rather tour Esopus Creek by rail, the railroad offers a 6-mile round-trip ride, stopping at Phoenicia at a circa 1900 train depot being restored by the Empire State Railway Museum.

Catskill Mountain Railroad Company, Route 28, Mount Pleasant 12457, (914) 688–7400, operates weekends and holidays Memorial Day weekend through mid-September with trains running hourly 11:00 A.M. to 5:00 P.M. Mid-September through mid-October, trains run weekends and holidays hourly from noon to 4:00 P.M. Fare is $6.00 round-trip for adults; $2.00 for children ages 4 to 11. Call ahead to verify schedules.

Mt. Pleasant is home to one of the Catskills' newest and most unusual tourist attractions—the ◆ **Kaatskill Kaleidoscope.** The 60-foot-high kaleidoscope, housed in the silo of a nineteenth-century barn, is the largest in the world. Charles Karadimos, one of the foremost creators of scopes, designed a 37-foot, pyramidal mirror assembly covered in a state-of-the-art reflective material. Isaac and Raphael Abrams (Isaac is sometimes referred to as the father of psychedelic fine art) came up with the theme of the kaleidoscope display: a journey through the history of America. Composer Gary Burke set the show to music. The result is a thirteen-minute sensory experience guaranteed to knock your socks off. The kaleidoscope won't be hard to find: Just look for a 60-foot blue silo with a painting of eyes on it, the work of Tibetan thanka painter Phuntsok Dorje.

The kaleidoscope is the centerpiece of **Catskill Corners,** a new complex celebrating Catskills life and attractions. **John Burroughs Park** is dedicated to the Catskill-born naturalist; his papers and writings are exhibited in the 1841 **Riseley Barn.** The **Longyear House,** home of the founder of the Ulster & Delaware Railroad, houses gallery exhibitions. The **Kaleidostore** features a large collection of scopes of every size, shape, and price range.

And, last but not least, the **Spotted Dog Firehouse Eatery,** a reproduction of a Victorian firehouse, has booths made from real fire engines and serves standard American fare at reasonable prices. Among the specialties are "Hellfire and Dalmation," a hot dog with a cup of three-alarm chili for $4.75; Esopus fish fry, native brook trout panfired with bacon and onions for $10.50; and "Backdraft," Catskill Corner's own special microbrew.

Catskill Corners, Route 28, Mt. Pleasant (Mt. Tremper) 12457, (914) 688–2451, kaleidoscope and complex are open 11:00 A.M. to 7:00 P.M. daily (closed Tuesday), and to 9:30 P.M. on Friday and Saturday nights. Admission is $5.00, and children under 4 are not admitted. The restaurant is open from noon to 9:30 P.M. daily, except Tuesday, (914) 688–7700.

Kaatskill Kaleidoscope

If you're looking for a more esoteric dining experience, **Catskill Rose** is an excellent option. How about appetizers such as potato Gruyère wedge with grilled portobello mushrooms, and entrees like chervil-stuffed broiled trout with lemon mustard and smoked duckling with strawberry rhubard sauce? The restaurant, on Route 212 in Mt. Tremper 12457, (914) 688-7100, begins serving dinner at 5:00 P.M. Wednesday through Sunday. Make reservations.

One of the country's first art colonies was founded in Woodstock in 1903, and today Ulster County is still a haven for artists. The **Woodstock Guild,** a multiarts center, displays and sells works of some of the area's best. It's at 34 Tinker Street, Woodstock 12498, (914) 679-2079 and is open daily 10:00 A.M. to 5:00 P.M.

There are numerous excellent restaurants in Woodstock. Among the more unusual is **New World Home Cooking Company,** 424 Zena Road, (914) 679-2600, featuring "New Wave" cooking—an eclectic assortment of ethnic dishes often pepped up with hot peppers and Asian spices. For example, it serves mussels with chili paste, or a Brie and pineapple quesadilla. There's a lovely outdoor patio and a great selection of beers to extinguish the fire. Open for lunch weekdays, dinner nightly, and Sunday brunch from April 30 through October. Reservations are a must on weekends.

Don't be misled by its name: In addition to a large selection of breads, **Bread Alone,** 22 Mill Hill Road, (914) 679-2108, bakes baguettes, coffeecakes, cheesecakes, cookies . . . the bakery/coffee shop is open daily from 7:30 A.M. to 6:00 P.M.

For almost forty years Harvey Fite has been creating a monumental environmental sculpture out of an abandoned Saugerties bluestore quarry. **◆ Opus 40,** made of hundreds of thousands of tons of finely fitted stone, covers more than six acres. Visitors can walk along its recessed lower pathways, around the pools and fountains, and up to the nine-ton monolith at the summit. To create his Opus, Fite worked with traditional tools that were used by quarrymen here. His Quarryman's Museum houses his collection of tools and artifacts.

Opus 40, High Woods, Saugerties 12477, (914) 246-3400, is open Memorial Day weekend through October, Fridays, Sundays, and some Saturdays (call in advance), noon to 5:00 P.M. Admission, which includes the museum, is $5.00 for adults, $4.00 for students and senior citizens, children under 12 free with adult.

If you've ever looked longingly at a distant lighthouse, wishing you could escape Wal-Mart, McDonald's, and the Internet for a bit, check into the ◆ **Saugerties Lighthouse,** a 130-year-old stone structure at the mouth of Esopus Creek on the Hudson River.

Deactivated by the U.S. Coast Guard in 1954, the lighthouse since been restored by the Saugerties Lighthouse Conservancy, which operates it as a museum and inn. In 1990 the Coast Guard installed a fourth-order solar-powered light, and the lighthouse once again aids mariners.

Two second-floor bedrooms are for rent. Guests share a kitchen with keeper Steve Thomas, who fabricated the lighthouse's interior trim. Guests get to the lighthouse via a half-mile nature trail (at low tide only) or by private boat.

The museum at Saugerties Lighthouse Conservancy, P.O. Box 654, Saugerties 12477, (914) 246–4380, is open Saturdays, Sundays, and holidays from 3:00 to 5:00 P.M. April through October. Advance reservations are required for rooms, which rent for $75 per night for two persons. There's a minimum charge of $150, which can be for a two-night stay or a one-night rental of both rooms.

New York's highest waterfall, 3 miles west of Tannersville, is no broad Niagara but more a miniature version of Angel Falls in Venezuela. **Kaaterskill Falls** leaps from a rock ledge as a narrow curtain of white water, plunging past a natural grotto to a second scooped-out shelf at which it gathers force to finish its plunge toward the floor of Kaaterskill Clove.

Now little celebrated outside of hikers' guidebooks, the falls was once the Catskills' most celebrated natural wonder. Thomas Cole, founder of the Hudson River School of art, immortalized the falls in his painting *View of Kaaterskill Falls* in the early 1800s.

The path to the base of the falls is not particularly difficult, although in the spring, when its snow cover has melted and refrozen into glare ice, it requires a gingerly step. But it is a short trail, and it follows the ravine gouged by Kaaterskill Creek for less than a mile before reaching the base. For the less adventurous or those who prefer viewing waterfalls from the top, there is a path to the head of the falls from the North/South Lake State Campground on Route 18, roughly 2 miles east of Haines Falls.

Now we're going to the Broncks. No, it's not the wrong chapter—or the wrong spelling. Bronck was the family name of one of the original clans of Swedish settlers in New Amsterdam and the Hudson Valley. The farmstead of Pieter Bronck, who settled on the west bank of the Hudson near what is now Coxsackie, today makes up the ◆ **Bronck Museum.**

It is one thing to have a surviving seventeenth-century house, but it is the great good fortune of the Greene County Historical Society, owner of the Bronck Museum, to be in possession of an entire farm dating from those early years of settlement. The reason the Bronck property has come down virtually intact is that eight generations of the family lived there, working the farm, until Leonard Bronck Lampman willed the acreage and buildings to the historical society. Thus, we get to appreciate not only the oldest of the farm buildings but also all of the barns, utility buildings, and furnishings acquired over two centuries of prosperity and familial expansion. What it all amounts to is an object lesson in the changes in style, taste, and sophistication that took place between the seventeenth and nineteenth centuries.

The Bronck Museum, Pieter Bronck Road, off Route 9W (mailing address: Greene County Historical Society, RD, Coxsackie 12051), (518) 731-8862 or 731-6490, is open from the last Sunday in June to the Sunday before Labor Day, Tuesday through Saturday, 10:00 A.M. to 5:00 P.M., and Sunday, 2:00 to 6:00 P.M.; Labor Day to October 15, Tuesday, Saturday, and Sunday, noon to 4:00 P.M..; and Columbus Day, noon to 4:00 P.M. Admission, including scheduled guided tours, is $4.00 for adults, $3.50 for senior citizens, $2.00 for children 12 to 15, and $1.00 for children 5 to 11. Group tours, by prior arrangement, are available from the end of May through the end of October.

UPPER CATSKILLS

If you're heading west from the Hudson Valley into the upper Catskills, a stop at the **Durham Center Museum** in East Durham provides an instructive look at the things a small community finds important—in many ways this museum is archetypical of the "village attics" that dot the land, and travelers could do worse than to take an occasional poke into one of these institutions. At the museum, which is housed in a circa 1825 one-room schoolhouse and several newer adjacent buildings, the collections run to Indian artifacts, portions of local petrified trees, old farm tools, and mementos of the 1800 Susquehanna Turnpike and the 1832–40 Canajoharie-Catskill Railroad, both of which passed this way. There is also a collection of Rogers Groups, those plaster statuette tableaux that decorated Victorian parlors and played on bourgeois heartstrings before Norman Rockwell was born. Finally, don't miss the collection of bottled sand specimens from around the world, sent by friends of the museum. If you're planning a trip to some far-off spot not represented on these shelves, don't hesitate to send some sand.

The Durham Center Museum, Route 145, East Durham 12423, (518) 239–4313 or 239–8461, is open June through August, Wednesday, Thursday, Saturday, and Sunday, from 1:00 to 4:00 P.M. Admission is $2.00

for adults and 50 cents for children under 12. Groups are welcome by appointment April through October. Genealogical researchers are welcome year-round by appointment.

While spending a summer day in East Durham, drop in at another local institution with a far more specialized collection—◆ **Richter's Butterfly Museum,** a small monument to one man's lifelong interest in lepidoptera. Max Richter was born in Germany, where even as a young boy he was fascinated with butterflies. When he moved to East Durham in 1932, he named his new country property Butterfly Farm. Here he raised butterflies, mounted them, and even made the mounted specimens into plaques. He opened his museum in 1953 and took great pride in showing his vast collection of butterflies to visitors over the next three decades. Mr. Richter passed away in 1984 at the age of 100, but his museum remains open under the curatorship of his daughter, Helen Richter Kruppenbacher. She presides over an expanded institution that even houses collections of beetles and seashells, along with a gift shop selling objets d'art made from real butterflies.

The Butterfly Museum, Wright Street, East Durham 12423, (518) 634–7759, is open during June, July, and August on Wednesday, Thursday, Saturday, and Sunday from 2:00 to 5:00 P.M.

In 1824 a young man named Zadock Pratt came to a settlement called Schoharie Kill to establish a tannery. He bought some land, surveyed it, and set up his factory. Over the next twenty years, more than 30,000 employees, using hides imported from South America, tanned a million sides of sole leather, which were shipped down the Hudson River to New York City. And in the meantime Mr. Pratt established Prattsville, one of the earliest planned communities in New York State.

Mr. Pratt went on to become a member of the U.S. Congress in 1836 and 1842. One of the bills he sponsored created the Smithsonian Institution, but one of the most enduring legacies he left behind was **Pratt Rock Park,** which he donated to the town in 1843. Carved into the park's cliffs are symbols of Mr. Pratt's life, including a huge bust of his son who was killed in the Civil War, a horse, a hemlock tree, an uplifted hand, his tannery, a wreath with the names of his children, and an unfinished tomb where Pratt was to be buried overlooking the village (he was buried in a conventional grave at the other end of town). There's also a grave site with a stone bearing the names of his favorite dogs and horses.

While you're in Prattsville, take time to visit the **Pratt Museum** (518-299-3395), located in Zadock Pratt's restored homestead in the center of town. The museum is just a half mile from the rocks; it's open May through October, Wednesday through Sunday, 1:00 to 5:00 P.M. There is an admission fee.

Roxbury, New York, is where we again come into contact with the naturalist John Burroughs. He may have spent much of the last decades of his life at Slabsides, down on the Hudson, but it was here in Roxbury that he was born in 1837 and here where he spent the last ten summers of his life at Woodchuck Lodge. He was buried here, in a field adjacent to the lodge, on April 2, 1921. The grave site and the nearby "Boyhood Rock" that he had cherished as a lad are now part of **Burroughs Memorial State Historic Site.**

The Burroughs Memorial is unique among historic sites, in that its chief feature (apart from the grave and the rock) is simply a field, surrounded by forests and the rolling Catskill hills. This is as fine a memorial as one could possibly imagine for a man who once said about the Catskills, "Those hills comfort me as no other place in the world does—it is home there."

Burroughs Memorial State Historic Site, off Route 30 (take Hardscrabble Road to Burroughs Road), Roxbury 12474, (315) 492–1756, is open during daylight hours from April to November 1. Admission is free. Woodchuck Lodge is frequently open to visitors on weekends during the summer.

Many of John Burroughs's modern-day spiritual descendants use the term *appropriate technology* to refer to renewable, nonpolluting sources of energy. Over in the northwestern Catskills town of East Meredith, the ◆ **Hanford Mills Museum** celebrates one of the oldest of these so-called alternative-energy sources, the power of running water harnessed to a wheel. Kortright Creek at East Meredith has been the site of waterpowered mills since the beginning of the nineteenth century, and the main building on the museum site today was built in 1846.

The old mill became the Hanford Mills in 1860, when David Josiah Hanford bought the operation. During the eighty-five years in which it owned the mill, the Hanford family expanded its output to include feed milling and the manufacture of utilitarian woodenware for farms and small industries. The mill complex grew to incorporate more than ten buildings on ten acres, all clustered around the millpond. The mill continued in operation until 1967.

Much of the original nineteenth-century equipment at Hanford Mills is still in place and in good working order. Today's visitors can watch lumber being cut on a big circular saw and shaped with smaller tools, all powered by the waters of Kortright Creek. At the heart of the operation is a 10-by-12-foot waterwheel, doing what waterwheels have done for more than 2,000 years.

The Hanford Mills Museum, intersection of County Routes 10 and 12, East Meredith 13757, (607) 278–5744, is open May 1 to October 31, daily, 10:00 A.M. to 5:00 P.M. Admission is $4.00 for adults and $2.50 for children. Senior citizens receive a discount. Group rates are available. Winter ice-harvesting programs are presented during January and February. Call for information.

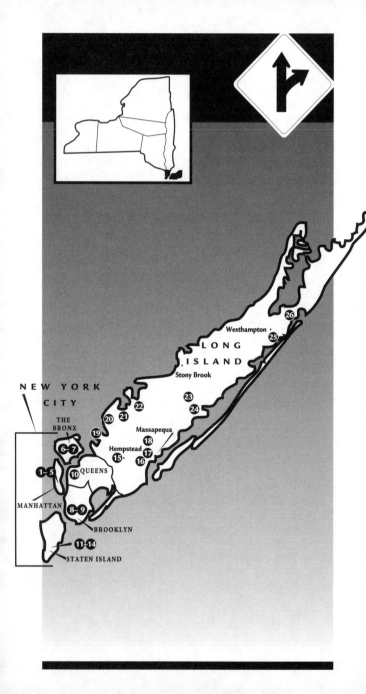

NEW YORK CITY AND LONG ISLAND

1. National Museum of the American Indian
2. African Burial Ground
3. Lower East Side Tenement Museum
4. Maxilla & Mandible, Ltd.
5. Black Fashion Museum
6. Poe Cottage
7. Wave Hill
8. Brooklyn Children's Museum
9. Aquarium for Wildlife Conservation
10. Isamu Noguchi Garden Museum
11. Jacques Marchais Museum of Tibetan Art
12. Historic Richmond Town
13. Staten Island Institute of Arts and Sciences
14. Alice Austen House
15. African American Museum
16. Nautical Mile
17. Dear Little Dollies
18. Old Bethpage Village Restoration
19. Sands Point Preserve
20. Holocaust Memorial and Educational Center of Nassau County
21. Planting Fields Arboretum
22. DNA Learning Center
23. American Armoured Foundation
24. Bayard Cutting Arboretum
25. 1880 House
26. Slo Jack's Miniature Golf

NEW YORK CITY AND LONG ISLAND

New York City needs no introduction—certainly not a cursory one of the length we're permitted here—except to note that this is where the most beaten of the state's paths converge. With one top-echelon attraction after another packed into the city, where do we find the lesser-known places of interest?

The answer is everywhere. One of the first things the traveler should realize about this city is that it is far more than a backdrop for the Statue of Liberty, the Metropolitan Museum of Art, Yankee Stadium, and their like. And natives often have to be reminded that New York isn't just a vast and cacophonous machine that reinvents itself daily. It is, in fact, a place with nearly 400 years of history, where Dutch farmers and quirky poets and future presidents have lived, and where people are concerned with Indian artifacts and Tibetan art and the minutiae of local history as well as with capital-C Culture.

As for Long Island, the main thing for people who don't live here to remember is that it's worth going to even if it isn't on the way to anything else. Starting near the city and heading east, we'll visit an assortment of historical sites and museums, along with places that remind us of the natural beauty and maritime flavor of Long Island before fast carpentry and fast food transformed so much of it into a vast suburb.

NEW YORK CITY

Looking for an offbeat tour of New York? Volunteers at **Big Apple Greeter** all have one thing in common: They know and love their city and want to share their knowledge—at no cost—with you. These volunteers are matched with visitors according to languages spoken and interests and will spend two to four hours showing you the neighborhoods throughout the five boroughs where New Yorkers live and work. They know where to find the best restaurants, flea markets, and lesser-known attractions.

Big Apple Greeter, 1 Centre Street, New York City 10007, (212) 669-2896, is a free public service. Be sure to contact them *at least* three business days in advance of your arrival; appointments are strictly subject to the availability of volunteers.

Bruce Kayton specializes in tours of another sort—**Radical Walking Tours.** He focuses on the progressive alternative history of places such as Greenwich Village, City Hall, Harlem, and Wall Street, where people like Emma Goldman, Sacco & Vanzetti, the Black Panthers, and Abbie Hoffman made their mark on the New York legend. Mr. Kayton conducts two Radical Walking Tours a month from March through December. Tours last two and one-half to three hours and the fee is $6.00. Call him at (718) 492-0069 for information.

River to River Downtown Tours offers yet another option. Several years ago lifelong Manhattan resident Ruth Alscher-Green—a former teacher—"traded in her ruler for a pair of Reeboks" and now conducts two-hour walking tours of Lower Manhattan, focusing on its art, architecture, and history. She's knowledgeable and enthusiastic—the aunt you always wish you had when you arrive in town. Ruth charges $35 per person, $50 for two, offers a special group rate, and will tailor her tour to your interests. Contact her after 9:00 A.M. at Apt. 19U, 375 South End Avenue, New York City 10280, (212) 321-2823.

Want to see what makes **Times Square** tick? A free **walking tour** leaves from the Times Square Visitors Center every Friday at noon.

Of all the first-rank museums in the city of New York—institutions that can lay justified claim to being the most comprehensive of their kind—perhaps the least well known is the ◆ **National Museum of the American Indian.** Nowhere else can we learn so much about the indigenous peoples who first called home the West Indies, North, Central, and South America.

George Heye was an heir to an oil fortune who early in his life worked as a railroad construction engineer in the Southwest. In 1897 he bought the first of his Indian artifacts, a contemporary Navajo buckskin shirt, and from that point went on to develop a collecting mania that encompassed all things native from Alaska to Tierra del Fuego. He bought items that had just been made (including, it is said, the clothes off Indians' backs), and he bought archaeological finds dating from long before the European discovery of America. Heye founded his museum in 1916, and it opened to the public six years later. At that stage the collector owned some four hundred thousand objects; today the museum has more than a million individual items.

Beaded Buckskin Dress
National Museum of the American Indian

Exhibits at the museum are arranged geographically, according to the regions inhabited by the major indigenous peoples of North America, the West Indies, Central America, and South America. Also, there are numerous items associated with individuals—Sitting Bull's war club, Crazy Horse's feather headdress, Geronimo's cane, among others. Much of the collection must be kept in storage, but the astounding variety of material that is on display should surely convince visitors that this is *the* museum of the peoples of the New World.

Throughout the year Native musicians, dancers, artists, and elders present both formal and informal programs designed to help visitors better understand Indian cultures.

The National Museum of the American Indian, Smithsonian Institution, Heye Center, Alexander Hamilton U.S. Custom House, One Bowling Green, New York City 10004, (212) 668–6624, or for recorded information (212) 825–6922, is open daily except Christmas from 10:00 A.M. to 5:00 P.M. and Thursday until 8:00 P.M. Admission is free.

New York's first Africans arrived in what is now Manhattan in a Dutch slave ship in 1626. A 1697 statute banned blacks from burying their dead in lower Manhattan churchyards, and an undesirable plot of land 2 blocks north of today's City Hall was designated for their use. It's estimated that between 1712 and 1794 some 10,000 to 20,000 people were buried there.

In 1991 archaeologists uncovered human bones beneath a vacant lot at 290 Broadway. Archaeologists called to the scene kept digging, and by the time they were done they had uncovered the remains of 425 Africans in what is believed to be one of—and perhaps, *the*—oldest and most extensive African burial sites in the country, the ◆ **African Burial Ground.** In 1993 the skeletal remains were shipped to Howard University in Washington, D.C., and are undergoing intensive analysis to help researchers glean information as to what the lives of blacks living in this area were like in the eighteenth century. Artifacts found at the site are being studied at a laboratory in the World Trade Center. Visitors can tour the laboratory (which is also doing research on a notorious eighteenth- and nineteenth-century lower Manhattan slum called Five Points), view a slide presentation about the excavation and its scientific implications, and tour the burial ground, designated both a New York City and federal landmark.

The African Burial Ground Project, Office of Public Education and Interpretation, 6 World Trade Center, Room 239, New York City 10048, (212) 432–5707, is open Monday through Friday, 10:00 A.M. to 6:00 P.M. and one Saturday each month. Admission and tours are free.

In the mid-1800s Lucas Glockner, a German-born tailor, bought a lot at 97 Orchard Street on the Lower East Side that measured 25 by 100 feet. The lot was originally intended for single-family townhouses, but Mr. Glockner erected a six-story tenement with apartments for twenty-two families as well as two storefronts in the basement. Each floor featured four three-room apartments with a total of 325 square feet each. Only one of the three rooms had windows.

Because it was the convention in the area for landlords to offer a free month's rent at the beginning of a year's lease, frequent moves were customary. Although 1,100 people have been documented as living at 97 Orchard Street between 1863 and 1935, a more realistic estimate is that 10,000 people from more than twenty-five nations lived at 97 Orchard Street during its seventy-two-year residential service.

Ninety-seven Orchard Street is the first tenement to be preserved in America, and it is the site of the ◆ **Lower East Side Tenement Museum,** whose mission is to "promote tolerance through the presentation and interpretation of the variety of urban immigrant experiences on Manhattan's Lower East Side, a gateway to America." Visitors see apartments restored to interpret the lives of the Gumpertzes, a German-Jewish family from the 1870s, and the Baldizzis, an Italian-Catholic family from 1935. The museum also hosts a series of weekend walks through the historic Orchard Street area. "The Streets Where We Lived" helps visitors learn how different immigrant groups shaped, and continue to shape, the Lower East Side.

All programs at the Lower East Side Tenement Museum, (212) 431-0233, begin at the Gallery, 90 Orchard Street, at the corner of Broome Street. The museum is open Tuesday through Sunday from 11:00 A.M. to 5:00 P.M. Call for specific tour times and admission fees. Free parking for the museum is available on Broome Street between Norfolk and Suffolk streets. Have your parking stub validated at the box office.

Back in Buffalo, a couple of chapters ago, we saw where the most momentous turn in Theodore Roosevelt's life took place—the house where he was inaugurated president of the United States. Here in the city you can see where his life began, at the **Theodore Roosevelt Birthplace National Historic Site.** The building that stands here today is a faithful reconstruction of the brownstone rowhouse in which TR was born on October 27, 1858. It was built following the ex-president's death in 1919, replacing a nondescript commercial building that had gone up only three years before, when the original Roosevelt home was torn down.

Qui Plantavit Curabit

The Roosevelt Arms
Theodore Roosevelt Birthplace

Open to the public since 1923, and a National Historic Site since 1963, the reconstructed Roosevelt home is furnished in the same style—and with many of the same articles—familiar to the sickly lad who lived here for the first fourteen years of his life. The president's widow and his two sisters supervised the reconstruction, recalling room layouts, furniture placement, and even interior color schemes. The result is a careful study not only of the environment that produced the scholar and improbable athlete who would become a rancher, police commissioner, Rough Rider, New York governor, and president, but also of the lifestyle of New York's more comfortable burghers in the middle of the last century. Finally, the "new" Roosevelt house stands in stubborn contrast to the modern buildings that surround it, reminding us of just how completely the neighborhoods of New York have thrown off one persona after another.

The Theodore Roosevelt Birthplace National Historic Site, 28 East Twentieth Street, New York City 10003, (212) 260-1616, is open Wednesday through Sunday, 9:00 A.M. to 5:00 P.M. Guided tours are given on the hour; last tour at 4:00 P.M. Closed on federal holidays. Admission is $2.00 for adults; seniors over 62 and children under 17 are admitted free. There is no charge for educational groups, but reservations must be made at least two weeks in advance.

There's no question that Americans are an industrious lot—New York City itself is a perfect example. But the fabulous collection of paintings, drawings, sculpture, textiles, furniture, functional and decorative arts, photographs, and contemporary environmental works on display at the **Museum of American Folk Art** is testament to the fact that man cannot live by bread alone—the soul, too, needs nurturing.

The museum, founded by a group of collectors in 1961, is devoted to preserving the country's rich folk heritage. The collection, dating from the middle eighteenth century to the present, reflects the museum's increasingly broad definition of the field of folk art. The museum presents special exhibitions and events throughout the year and publishes *Folk Art* magazine, the only publication in the country covering the growing field of American folk art.

The Museum of American Folk Art, Two Lincoln Square (Columbus Avenue between Sixty-fifth and Sixty-sixth streets), New York City 10023, (212) 595-9533, is open Tuesday through Sunday, 11:30 A.M. to 7:30 P.M. Closed Monday. Admission is free.

Looking for an unusual souvenir? Perhaps the horn of an impala (*Aepyceros melampus*), the skeleton of the Look Down fish (*Selene vomer*), or the skull of a Tokay Gecko (*Gecko gecko*) will do. ◆ **Maxilla & Mandible, Ltd.,** the world's only osteological store, is a natural history and science emporium with 19,000 square feet of showroom, laboratory, workshop, and storage facilities. All of their specimens are unique, anatomically accurate, and obtained from legal and ethical sources. They're at 451-5 Columbus Avenue, New York City, 10024, (212) 724-6173, and are open Monday through Saturday, 11:00 A.M. to 7:00 P.M., and Sunday, 1:00 to 5:00 P.M. Request a catalog—it's the *Felis catus*'s pajamas.

The ◆ **Black Fashion Museum** is the only one in the country devoted to acknowledging the fashion achievments and contributions of black people. In 1978 founder Lois K. Alexander traveled across the country collecting garments and memorabilia. She states, "the purpose of the museum is to correct the misapprehension that black Americans are newfound talent in the fashion industry."

The collection contains items dating back to 1865—including two authentic slave dresses and a copy of Mary Todd Lincoln's inaugural gown; five gowns by Ann Lowe, who designed Jacqueline

Bouvier's gown for her wedding to John F. Kennedy; a dress made by Rosa Parks; and costumes from Broadway musicals such as "The Wiz" and "Bubbling Brown Sugar." Also in the collection are fashions from contemporary designers such as Geoffrey Holder, Harold Stone, and Zelda Wynn. In addition the museum mounts two special exhibitions each year.

The Black Fashion Museum, 155 West 126th Stret, New York City 10027, (212) 666-1320, is open by appointment Wednesday through Saturday from 11:00 A.M. to 6:00 P.M. Admission is charged.

Harlem . . . a place rich in history, tradition, food, music, and bad press . . . where the majority of people go about their daily lives in peace, but tourists are usually too apprehensive to visit. An enterprising company called **Harlem Spirituals** now gives tours of uptown Manhattan, and visitors can enjoy all of the sights with peace of mind. The "Harlem on Sunday" tour includes a visit to a church service, complete with gospel music, and a stop at the historic high spots. If you opt for Sunday brunch, you'll end the morning with soul food and gospel music at the famous Cotton Club. Harlem Spirituals also offers weekday tours—which include stops at the Apollo Theater, souvenir shops, and the Addicts Rehabilitation Center to listen to the ARC Gospel Choir—and evening "Soul Food and Jazz" tours.

Harlem Spirituals, 1697 Broadway, #203, New York City 10019, (212) 757-0425, offers tours in English, French, German, Italian, and Spanish, as well as other languages, based on availability.

It's 3:00 A.M. and you've got the hungry horrors. A few places in the Big Apple that never close include **Bialy Kosher,** 367 Grand Street, (212) 674-9747 for take-out bagels; **Hong Fat,** 63 Mott Street, (212) 962-9588 for take-out; **Kiev,** 117 Second Avenue, (212) 674-4040 for homemade soups, dumplings, and blintzes; and **Original Ray's,** 835 Seventh Avenue at 53rd, (212) 974-9381 for fresh-baked pizza.

And now, on to the U.S. mainland—to the only borough of the city of New York not located on an island. This is the Bronx, a place that ought to be recognized as more than the home of Yankee Stadium and the place you cross on Route 95 to get from New England to the George Washington Bridge. To get a handle on the story of this one-time suburban retreat that became one of New York's most densely populated residential districts, visit the **Museum of Bronx History.** The museum is housed in a building of a style and period not often encountered in a city that has torn down and rebuilt itself with as much abandon as has New York—a fieldstone house built in 1758, looking as if it would be more at home on a farm in Bucks County, Pennsylvania, than in the borough of endless rowhouses and apartment buildings.

The Museum of Bronx History, 3266 Bainbridge Avenue at 208th Street, Bronx 10467, (718) 881-8900, is open Saturday from 10:00 A.M. to 4:00 P.M., Sunday from 1:00 to 5:00 P.M., and weekdays from 9:00 A.M. to 5:00 P.M. by appointment. Admission is $2.00.

One chapter in Bronx history is an important part of American literary history as well. In 1846 a thirty-seven-year-old poet, short story writer, and critic named Edgar Allan Poe rented a small wooden cottage now known as the ◆ **Poe Cottage,** in Poe Park, East Kingsbridge Road and the Grand Concourse, not far from the campus of Fordham University (in Poe's day it was known as St. John's College). Part of the reason for his move was the fragile health of his wife; Fordham, Poe thought, was a more salubrious environment than the couple's former home in New York City. But Virginia Clemm Poe—who was also the writer's cousin—died of tuberculosis at the Bronx cottage early in 1847, leaving Poe in the state of despondency that accounted for his poem "Annabel Lee" and other melancholic verse.

Poe maintained his residence in the Bronx after his wife's death, drinking heavily and trying to keep up with his bills by delivering an occasional lecture. It was while returning from one of his lecture trips that he died in Baltimore in 1849.

Sometimes the world takes better care of dead poets' residences than it does the poets while they are alive, and such was the case with Edgar Allan Poe. The rapidly growing Bronx quickly enveloped the Poe Cottage during the latter half of the nineteenth century, but in 1902 the city dedicated a park in his honor across the street from the house. The house was moved to the park eleven years later and has been open as a museum since 1917.

The Edgar Allan Poe Cottage, Grand Concourse and East Kingsbridge Road, Bronx 10458, (718) 881-8900, is open Saturday, 10:00 A.M. to 4:00 P.M., and Sunday, 1:00 to 5:00 P.M. throughout the year. Admission is $2.00 for adults and $1.00 for children under 12.

Not all of the Bronx was gobbled up by developers in the decades following Poe's brief stay. There are, of course, the green expanses of the New York Botanical and Zoological Gardens, Van Cortlandt Park, and Pelham Bay Park. But a visit to the borough should also include a stop at ◆ **Wave Hill,** a twenty-eight-acre preserve in the Riverdale neighborhood at the northwest corner of the Bronx. Wave Hill is not wilderness but a section of the borough that remained in its natural state until the middle of the last century, when it was first acquired as a country estate. Today it is the only one of the great Hudson River estates preserved for public use within the city limits.

In 1836 New York lawyer William Morris bought fifteen acres of riverbank real estate in the Wave Hill area and built Wave Hill House, one of the two mansions that today grace the property, as a summer retreat. Thirty years later the Morris tract was acquired by publisher William Appleton. Appleton remodeled the house and began developing the gardens and conservatories for which the property would become famous. The gardens were brought to their apogee, however, by financier George Perkins, who bought the estate in 1893 and increased its size to eighty acres, with a scattering of six fine houses, including not only Wave Hill but also **Glyndor,** which had been built by Oliver Harriman. (Burned in 1927, Glyndor was rebuilt by Perkins's widow. Glyndor II, as it is known, is still a part of the Wave Hill property.) Perkins's gardener was the talented Albert Millard. Under his direction plantings on the estate were expanded to include eight additional greenhouses and exotic Oriental trees.

The attractions of Wave Hill for today's visitor include art exhibits, concert series, outdoor dance performances, and special events. But the essential reason for a trip to the old estate remains its lovely grounds, some manicured and some an approximation of the wild state of this stretch of Bronx shoreline. There are 350 varieties of trees and shrubs, plus the wild and cultivated flowers planted in three greenhouses, in formal and informal gardens, and along the pathways of the estate. A ten-acre section of woods has been restored as a native Bronx forest environment, complete with elderberries, witch hazel, and native grasses.

Wave Hill, 249th Street and Independence Avenue, Bronx (mailing address: 675 West 252nd Street, Bronx 10471), (718) 549–3200, is open daily, 9:00 A.M. to 4:30 P.M.; closed Christmas and New Year's Day. Admission is free weekdays; on Saturdays and Sundays it is $4.00 for adults, $2.00 for seniors and students, and free for children 6 and under. Tours are given each Sunday.

The kids have been great. They've listened to you quote stanzas from "The Raven" and heard about Teddy Roosevelt's charge up San Juan Hill. So now head over to the **Brooklyn Children's Museum.** Founded in 1899, it was the first museum in the world designed expressly for youngsters. It will give you a chance to stop worrying about them touching everything—here the philosophy is "touch and learn."

The museum, with a collection of more than 27,000 artifacts and specimens, is housed in a unique, 35,000-

square-foot underground structure and features a turn-of-the-century kiosk entrance and a "stream" running the length of the "people tube," a huge drainage pipe that connects four levels of exhibit space. According to the museum's brochure, "exhibits combine 'hands- on' components and objects to aid in the exploration of natural science, culture and history"—which translates to "learn and have fun at the same time."

Among the latest additions/renovations are a rooftop amphitheatre and a greenhouse, created jointly with the Brooklyn Botanic Garden. A trolley-to-shuttle service between the Children's Museum, Brooklyn Museum, and the Botanic Garden is scheduled to begin operation in the spring of 1997.

The Brooklyn Children's Museum, 145 Brooklyn Avenue, Brooklyn 11213, (718) 735–4400, is open during the school year Wednesday through Friday, 2:00 to 5:00 P.M. and Saturday and Sunday, noon to 5:00 P.M.; and during July and August, Monday, Wednesday, Thursday, Saturday, and Sunday, noon to 5:00 P.M. and Friday, noon to 6:30 P.M. There is a suggested contribution of $3.00 per visitor.

The Wildlife Conservation Society's ◆ **Aquarium for Wildlife Conservation,** on Brooklyn's Coney Island, is the oldest continuously operating aquarium in the country. It houses more than 10,000 specimens, including the only California sea otters outside of California, and the only aquarium-born beluga whales to survive past their first birthday.

In 1993 the aquarium opened Sea Cliffs, a 300-foot-long re-creation of the rocky Pacific coast, now home to walruses; harbor, grey, and fur seals; sea otters; and black-footed penguins. Exhibits in Conservation Hall focus on the society's efforts to protect marine species around the world, replicating habitats in areas such as the Belize Barrier Reef, the Amazon River, the Coral Reef, and Lake Victoria. The new Aquatheater features a 200,000-gallon pool where marine mammal demonstrations are held throughout the day.

The Aquarium for Wildlife Conservation, Boardwalk at West Eighth Street and Surf Avenue, Coney Island, Brooklyn 11224, (718) 265–FISH, opens daily at 10:00 A.M. and closes at 5:00 P.M. on weekdays and at 7:00 P.M. summer weekends and holidays Memorial Day through Labor Day. Admission is $7.75 for adults and $3.50 for senior citizens and children ages 2 to 12.

"It is said that stone is the affection of old men," said American-Japanese sculptor Isamu Noguchi, explaining his obsession with the medium. Caress the smooth, cold stone of his pieces, and perhaps you'll understand. They're displayed in the Long Island City neighborhood of the borough of Queens at the ◆ **Isamu Noguchi Garden Museum,** a brick factory building the artist converted for use as a warehouse in the 1970s. Prior to the museum's opening, he added a dramatic open-air addition and an outdoor sculpture garden. Today more than 250 of his works, including stone, bronze, and wood sculptures; models for public projects and gardens; elements of dance sets designed for choreographer Martha Graham; and his Akari lanterns are exhibited in twelve galleries in the building.

Mr. Noguchi's major granite and basalt sculptures are displayed in the garden, as is his tombstone, under which half of his ashes are interred. The other half is buried in his garden studio in Japan.

The Isamu Noguchi Garden Museum, 32-37 Vernon Boulevard, Long Island City 11106, (718) 204-7088, is open April through October, Wednesday through Friday, 10:00 A.M. to 5:00 P.M., and Saturday and Sunday, 11:00 A.M. to 6:00 P.M. There is a suggested contribution of $4.00 for adults and $2.00 for senior citizens and students. A free gallery tour is provided daily at 2:00 P.M. On weekends the museum operates a shuttle-bus service from Manhattan. Call for information.

The borough of Queens is New York's most residential neighborhood—or rather, collection of neighborhoods, each retaining its own distinctive character. One such neighborhood is Flushing, best known to many non-native New Yorkers as the site of the 1939 and 1964 World's Fairs. The history of this district goes back well over 300 years, as a visit to the **Bowne House** will demonstrate.

John Bowne built the house that today bears his name in 1661. To get some idea of what the future outlying boroughs of New York were like in those days, consider that two years after the Bowne House was built, the town meeting of nearby Jamaica offered a bounty of seven bushels of corn for every wolf shot or otherwise done away with. But wolves weren't the only threat John Bowne faced. A Quaker, he openly challenged Governor Peter Stuyvesant's edict banning that religion by holding meetings of the Society of Friends in his kitchen. He was arrested and sent back to Europe in 1662 but came back to New York two years later, after having been exonerated by the Dutch West India Company, managers of the New Amsterdam colony.

Now the oldest house in Queens, the Bowne House reflects not only the Dutch/English Colonial style in which it was originally built but also all of the vernacular styles with which it was modified over the years.

The Bowne House displays styles of furnishing and portrait painting as they developed over the first two centuries of its existence. Everything here belonged to the Bownes, making this property a unique documentation of one family's experience in New York virtually from the time of its founding to the beginning of the modern era.

The Bowne House, 37-01 Bowne Street, Flushing 11354, (718) 359-0528, is open Tuesday, Saturday, and Sunday, 2:30 to 4:30 P.M.; closed major holidays and mid-December to mid-January. Admission is $2.00 for adults and $1.00 for children. Groups welcome by appointment.

In 1694 the Friends of Flushing Village—now a part of Queens— moved their meeting out of member John Bowne's house to a newly erected **Quaker Meeting House.** By 1717 the membership had grown so large that the Quakers built an addition doubling the size of the original structure. Since then the house has remained virtually unchanged—a perfectly preserved early American structure still being used as its builders intended.

The Quaker Meeting House, 137-16 Northern Boulevard, Flushing 11357, (718) 358–9636, is open for worship every Sunday from 11:00 A..M. to noon. Tours are conducted after worship from noon to 1:00 P.M. Group and school tours are by appointment.

Queens Historical Society has designed a self-guiding **Flushing Freedom Mile Historic Tour** encompassing nineteen historic sites, including the Bowne House and the Quaker Meeting House. For a copy write them at 143-35 Thirty-seventh Avenue, Flushing 11354.

A seventeenth-century Quaker going to a clandestine meeting at the Bowne House might seem to have little in common with a twentieth-century Tibetan Buddhist, but the two share a bond of persecution. One of the uglier aspects of the Maoist period in China was the annexation of Tibet and the suppression of its ancient culture and religion. Despite some recent liberalization on the part of the Chinese occupiers of Tibet, it is still an extremely difficult place to visit; and ironically, those Westerners interested in Tibetan art and religious artifacts have learned to rely on foreign rather than native Tibetan collections. One such collection is the ◆**Jacques Marchais Museum of Tibetan Art** on Staten Island. The museum houses more than a thousand examples of Tibetan religious art—paintings, carved and cast statues, altars, ritual objects, and musical instruments—each of which was created to aid in the meditation that is such an important part of Buddhism, especially as practiced in Tibet.

And who was Jacques Marchais? "He" was a woman

Crowned Buddha
Jacques Marchais Museum of Tibetan Art

named Jacqueline Coblentz Klauber who operated a
Manhattan art gallery under the masculine French
pseudonym. Klauber/Marchais had a lifelong interest
in things Tibetan that she said originated in her childhood when she would play with Tibetan figures her
great-grandfather had brought back from the Orient.
She never traveled to Tibet, but she carefully added to
her collection until her death in 1947.

With its terraced gardens, lily pond, and air of

detachment and serenity, the Marchais Museum is indeed an appropriate setting for the religious objects that make up the collection, representing centuries of Tibetan culture.

The Jacques Marchais Museum of Tibetan Art, 338 Lighthouse Avenue, Staten Island 10306, (718) 987-3500, is open 1:00 to 5:00 P.M. Wednesday through Sunday, from mid-April to November; December through March, by appointment. Closed Memorial Day, July 4, Labor Day, Thanksgiving Day, and the Friday following Thanksgiving Day. Admission is $3.00 for adults, $2.50 for senior citizens, and $1.00 for children. Group tours are available by appointment.

Within walking distance of the Marchais Museum is a collection of buildings representative of cultural continuity rather than upheaval and transplanting. ◆ **Historic Richmond Town** is a collection of twenty-seven buildings, fourteen of them restored and open to the public on a seasonal basis, that reminds us that Staten Island has a richer history than might be suggested by the tract houses and refineries that characterize the present-day borough of Richmond.

Richmond Town seems like a country village far from the bustle of Manhattan, and with good reason—that's what it was, in the seventeenth and eighteenth centuries when these houses and community buildings were built. Among them are the "Voorlezer's [Teacher's] House," a Dutch-era one-room school; an old county courthouse; a general store; and a farmhouse. Many of the buildings are staffed by craftspeople working with period equipment. White clapboard farmhouses dot the property's 100 acres, and a central museum houses exhibits of Staten Island–made products that reveal the history and diversity of New York's least populous borough. There are special events through the year, and nineteenth-century dinners are served during the summer.

Historic Richmond Town, 441 Clark Avenue, Staten Island 10306, (718) 351–1611, is open Wednesday through Sunday, 1:00 to 5:00 P.M. Closed weekends in January, February, and March. Hours are extended in July and August. Admission is $4.00 for adults and $2.50 for students, senior citizens, and children 6 to 18.

The oldest cultural institution on Staten Island is the ◆ **Staten Island Institute of Arts and Sciences,** founded in 1881 and headquartered in the small community of St. George just 2 blocks from the Staten Island Ferry Terminal. The institute's collection has been described as "eclectic"—and eclectic it is. Exhibits focus on the art, natural science, and cultural history of Staten Island and its people, drawing from the institute's collections of more than two million artifacts and specimens.

The art collection includes many fine works from ancient to contemporary periods, including works by Staten Island artists such as Jasper Cropsey, Guy Pene duBois, and Cecil Bell. Also included are pieces by internationally acclaimed talents such as Marc Chagall, Reginald Marsh, and Robert Henri, as well as decorative arts, furniture, clothing, and more. The natural history collections include 500,000 insects, 25,000 plant specimens, and geologic, shell, and archaeological specimens. The archives and library comprise the largest holdings of Staten Island history and science anywhere. Public programs for all ages include weekly "Lunch & Learn" buffets.

The Staten Island Institute of Arts and Sciences, 75 Stuyvesant Place, Staten Island 1030l, (718) 727–1135, is open Monday through Saturday, 9:00 A.M. to 5:00 P.M., and Sunday, 1:00 to 5:00 P.M. Suggested admission is $2.50 for adults and $1.50 for students and senior citizens. Parking behind the institute is available. Special tours and programs, including gallery tours, guided ferry rides, St. George walking tours, and formal classroom programs, are available to groups.

The best bargain in New York City is a 50-cent, round-trip, 5-mile ride aboard the Staten Island Ferry and then a visit to the **Staten Island Ferry Collection of the Staten Island Institute of Arts and Sciences** at St. George Terminal, just a short distance from the institute.

The ride aboard the ferry offers a complete view of the harbor, including the Brooklyn Bridge, Manhattan skyline, Statue of Liberty, Ellis Island, Governors Island, Robin's Reef Lighthouse, and the Verrazano-Narrows Bridge. The Staten Island Ferry Collection's exhibition explores the history of the ferry line and New York Harbor using striking displays of artifacts and photographs.

The Staten Island Ferry Collection of the Staten Island Institute of Arts and Sciences, St. George Terminal, Staten Island 10301, (718) 727–1135, is open Monday through Friday, 10:00 A.M. to 3:00 P.M.;

Saturday, 10:00 A.M. to 4:00 P.M.; and Sunday, 11:00 A.M. to 4:00 P.M. Admission is $1 for adults and 25 cents for children 12 and under.

Clear Comfort, one of the picturesque suburban "cottages" that dotted the shoreline of nineteenth-century Staten Island, was the home of Alice Austen (1866–1952), one of the country's first women photographers. The house was extensively renovated by her father, John, over a period of twenty-five years. By the time he was finished, he had transformed the rundown eighteenth-century Dutch farmhouse into a magnificently landscaped Carpenter Gothic cottage.

Alice lived in the house until illness and financial problems forced her to move in 1945. In the 1960s a group of citizens launched a successful effort to save Clear Comfort, and an exact restoration based on hundreds of Ms. Austen's photographs was completed in 1985. The home was designated a New York City Landmark in 1971 and a National Historic Landmark in 1993.

Today the gingerbread-gabled home overlooking the Narrows—the shipping channel for the Port of New York—serves as a gallery for her wonderful photographs documenting life in turn-of-the-century America. Changing exhibitions exploring themes inspired by her work and times often use images from the Staten Island Historical Society's Alice Austen Collection of nearly 3,000 negatives. A video narrated by Helen Hayes tells the story of *Alice's World*.

The ◆ **Alice Austen House,** 2 Hylan Boulevard, Staten Island 10305, (718) 816–4506, is open Thursday through Sunday, noon to 5:00 P.M. and closed major holidays. There is a suggested donation of $2.00.

LONG ISLAND

East of New York City, beyond the borders of the boroughs of Brooklyn and Queens, Long Island stretches from the populous cities and towns of Nassau County to the beaches and New England–style villages of Suffolk County. Beginning in the Nassau County city of Hempstead, our first stop is the ◆**African American Museum.**

Founded in 1970 under the auspices of the Nassau County Department of Recreation and Parks in response to growing awareness of the contributions of blacks on Long Island, the Black History Exhibit Center recently changed its name to the African American Museum and altered its emphasis to include interpretive exhibits of traditional and contemporary native African culture as well as local American black history and lore.

The black experience in New York State is by no means concentrated in New York City; nor is it a phenomenon largely associated with twentieth-century migrations from the South. A hundred years ago and more, blacks were farming, whaling, and working at crafts and small businesses on Long Island. Their ancestry, in many cases, dated back to the seventeenth- and eighteenth-century days when slavery—though not as widespread as it would become in the South—was still practiced in New York and the New England states.

The African American Museum tells the story of Long Island's blacks through displays of photographs and artifacts, lectures, workshops, and performing arts. Local artistic talent is especially promoted. African-oriented exhibits and special programs have included shows devoted to West African crafts, art from Sierra Leone, African toys, and black artistic expression in South Africa.

The African American Museum, 110 North Franklin Street, Hempstead 11550, (516) 572-0730, is open Thursday through Saturday, 10:00 A.M. to 4:45 P.M., and Sunday, 1:00 to 4:45 P.M. Admission is free.

Another Hempstead attraction is not really in Hempstead but in the south-shore village of Lawrence, just across the New York City limits from Far Rockaway, Queens. This is **Rock Hall Museum,** a 1767 mansion built by Tory merchant Josiah Martin.

Rock Hall represents the high-water mark of late Georgian architecture in this part of the country, particularly in its interior detailing. The paneling and mantels, as well as much of the eighteenth- and early nineteenth-century furniture and the replica of a colonial kitchen (the original kitchen was in an outbuilding), came down virtually unchanged to our own time. Josiah Martin's family, having come through the revolution none the worse for being on the wrong side, lived here until 1823. The following year Thomas Hewlett bought Rock Hall; his family lived in the mansion for more than a century after his death in 1841. In 1948 the Hewletts gave the place to the town of Hempstead—presumably then a larger municipal entity—for use as a museum.

Rock Hall Museum, 199 Broadway, Lawrence 11559, (516) 239-1157, is open April 1 through November 30 on Monday and on Wednesday through Saturday, 10:00 A.M. to 4:00 P.M.; on Sunday hours are noon to 4:00 P.M. Closed Tuesday. Admission is free.

With 8.5 miles of waterfront, Freeport calls itself "The Boating and Fishing Capital of the East." Woodcleft Avenue, informally known as ◆**Nautical Mile,** is rumored to have once been a haven for bootleggers, pirates, and other scoundrels. Today it is a mecca for sightseers, browsers, and seafood lovers. Restaurants, pubs, fish markets, and gift shops line the avenue, and one of the Island's largest charter/sport fishing fleets sails out of the harbor daily in season.

If your idea of dolls begins and ends with Barbie and Ken, expand your horizons with a visit to ◆**Dear Little Dollies.** More than 5,000 dolls fill every nook and cranny of the 5,000-square-foot store. Barbie is here—but so are one-of-a-kind dolls and limited editions by contemporary artists such as Yolanda Bello and Paul Crees; ethnic dolls; and mid-priced dolls from makers including Seymour Mann, Kingstate, and Ashton-Drake Galleries. Prices range from $20 to $14,000. Dorothy and Louis Camilleri, owners of Dear Little Dollies, host numerous artist signings in the shop and Meet-the-Artist Sunday brunches in the restaurant next door (by invitation only). They also offer a mail order service.

Dear Little Dollies, 418 Bedford Avenue, Bellmore 11710, (516) 679-0164, is open daily.

On Long Island's south shore in Seaford is a museum and preserve dedicated to life on the island as it was lived even before the era of farm and village life.

The **Tackapausha Museum and Preserve** is an eighty-acre introduction to the ecology and natural history of the Northeast's coastal woodlands. Tackapausha is named after a sachem (chief) of Long Island's native Massapequa Indians, a group that by and large managed to live on this land without greatly affecting its wildlife, its plant communities, or the balance of natural forces.

The Tackapausha Museum is a small facility designed to serve as an introduction to the plants and animal life of the preserve itself. Exhibits explain the relationship between habitat groups, the differences between diurnal and nocturnal animals, and the changes in life patterns brought about by the different seasons. There is also a small collection of native animals, housed in as natural a setting as possible.

The preserve itself is a lovely piece of land, incorporating a variety of ecosystems. A self-guiding trail (pick up the interpretive map at the museum) takes visitors through the different environments.

The Tackapausha Museum and Preserve, Washington Avenue, Seaford 11783, (516) 571-7443, is open Tuesday through Saturday, 10:00 A.M. to 4:00 P.M., and Sunday, 1:00 to 4:00 P.M. Admission is $1.00 for adults, 50 cents for children 5 or older, and free for children under 5.

For forty-one years the folks at **Krish** have been serving up great food and delicious homemade ice cream and candies. Chase down a scoop of cookie dough or peach with a fabulous chocolate truffle. It's all at 11 Central Avenue in Massapequa and is open daily from 7:30 A.M. to 11:00 P.M.

At our next stop we find plentiful evidence of the relentless trend toward suburbanization that has characterized this place during the past forty years. But we also find an institution that has set as its goal the preservation of as much as possible of the old, rural Long Island way of life. ◆ **Old Bethpage Village Restoration** is a re-creation of the world as it was long before there was a Levittown or Long Island Expressway. In fact—at least as far as its buildings are concerned—it is the architectural equivalent of a wildlife preserve.

**Quilting in the Noon Inn
Old Bethpage Village Restoration**

Starting in the middle 1960s, the curators of the village (it's managed by the Nassau County Department of Recreation and Parks) began moving threatened colonial and early nineteenth-century structures here, where they could be set up in a close approximation of a Long Island village of the Civil War era. There are now nearly fifty buildings on the site, all of them having been chosen to represent typical domestic, commercial, and agricultural structures of the era.

All of those buildings without people and activity would make for a rather dry museum, so Old Bethpage Village has been staffed with historically attired guides and craftspeople. There's even an Old Bethpage Village militia, which will presumably come in handy if the place is ever attacked by a contingent from the Genesee Country Village or the Farmers' Museum at Cooperstown.

Old Bethpage Village Restoration, Round Swamp Road, Old Bethpage 11804, (516) 572–8400 (recorded message) or 572–8401, is open Wednesday through Sunday from 10:00 A.M. to 5:00 P.M. March through December. Closed January and February. Admission is $5.00 for adults and $3.00 for children and senior citizens (prices subject to change). Closed holidays except Memorial Day, July 4, Labor Day, and Columbus Day, when the restoration is closed the day after. Call for information on the holiday candlelight evenings.

The **Gold Coast,** up on the north shore of Long Island, was created during the Roaring Twenties by families such as the Vanderbilts, the Chryslers, the Phippses, the Woolworths, and the Guggenheims, who built great mansions there.

For information on which ones are open to the public for tours call the **Long Island Convention and Visitors Bureau,** (800) 441–4601.

◆ **Sands Point Preserve** overlooking Long Island Sound has something for both mansion and nature lovers. A large portion of the 216-acre property was owned by railroad heir Howard Gould at the turn of the century. He built the Tudor-inspired **Hempstead House** and **Castlegould,** the enormous turreted stable and carriage house that now serve as a visitor center. In 1917 the Daniel Guggenheim family purchased the estate, and in 1923 Harry Guggenheim, Daniel's son, built the Norman mansion **Falaise** (the French word for cliff) on his share of the family property.

Today the property is owned by the Nassau County Department of Recreation and Parks, which preserves it not only as a focus of historical interest but also for the preservation and public enjoyment of its natural surroundings. Castlegould features large traveling natural history exhibits that change twice a year, plus the Dinosaur and Mammal Menagerie with fossils and interactive exhibits. There are six marked nature trails; two of them are self-guiding, and one follows the shoreline. In addition to numerous geological phenomena, such as glacial erratics (large granite boulders dropped from the ice during the last continental glaciation about 20,000 years ago), there is a wide range of plant and bird life within the preserve. Kids will enjoy following the special Dinosaur Trail, with its replicas of real fossilized dinosaur tracks. Pick up trail maps at the visitor center in Castlegould.

Sands Point Preserve, 95 Middleneck Road, Port Washington 11050, (516) 571-7900, is open year-round, Tuesday through Sunday, from 10:00 A.M. until 5:00 P.M. Falaise and Hempstead House are open for guided tours Wednesday through Sunday from May through October, call for times. There is a charge for special natural history exhibits in Castlegould and a separate charge for tours of Falaise and Hempstead House.

The ◆Holocaust Memorial & Educational Center of Nassau County, on the 204-acre Welwyn Preserve, hopes to "foster a greater understanding of the causes and consequences of one of the darkest periods in world history." The center hosts ongoing exhibits and has a 1,850-volume library. It's at 100 Crescent Beach Road in Glen Cove 11542, (516) 571-8040, and is open Monday through Friday, 10:00 A.M. to 4:00 P.M., and Sunday, 11:00 A.M. to 4:00 P.M. Admission is free.

◆Planting Fields Arboretum is the legacy of William Robertson Coe, a British-born insurance magnate who purchased this property in 1913. Coe immediately set about making his 409-acre estate into as complete a farm-garden-arboretum as possible. He began building greenhouses in 1914 (Coe Hall, the great house on the property, did not go up until 1919-21) and imported his camellia collection in 1917. The camellias couldn't make it through a Long Island winter, so a special greenhouse was built for them. Coe set up a working dairy and kept pigs and chickens as well. (Milk and produce from Planting Fields were donated to the needy during the Great Depression.)

But it was trees and shrubs that most commanded Coe's attention, and they were the subject of some of his greatest extravagances. The copper beech on the north lawn, for instance, was moved here from Massachusetts by barge and a team of seventy-two horses when it was already 60 feet high. Working with master landscape gardeners such as A. Robeson Sargent and James Dawson of Olmsted Brothers, Coe created grand allées of trees designed to frame the views from the house, and he established rambling azalea walks. As late as the 1950s, in the last years of his life, Coe planted the rhododendron park, which remains one of the outstanding features of Planting Fields.

There are concerts in the Haybarn (write for a schedule), and from April through September visitors can tour Coe Hall Monday through Friday and Sunday, 12:30 to 3:30 P.M. The fee is $3.50 for adults and children over 12, $2.00 for seniors, $1.00 for children ages 7 to 12, and those under 7 are free.

Planting Fields Arboretum, Box 58 (off Mill River Road), Oyster Bay 11771, (516) 922–9200, is open daily, 9:00 A.M. to 5:00 P.M. There is a $4.00 entry charge per car daily from May 4 through Labor Day and a $4.00 entry charge per car from Labor Day through the end of April on Saturday, Sunday, and holidays.

> Tis advertised in Boston, New York and Buffalo,
> Five hundred brave Americans a-whaling for to go,
> Singing "Blow, ye winds in the morning,
> Blow ye winds heigh-o,
> Heave away, haul away, and blow, winds, blow."

So goes the old chantey.

But where would these brave whalers ship out from once they had answered the call? Most often they would go down to the sea at New Bedford or Nantucket; if they began their hard voyages on Long Island, most likely their home port would be Sag Harbor. But there were also smaller whaling ports on Long Island, such as Cold Spring Harbor. Here today the **Whaling Museum** celebrates the skills and adventures of the town's own whalers as well as those of other men who worked in this arduous industry from colonial times through the nineteenth century.

The Whaling Museum houses a large collection of the implements used in the whale "fishery," as it was

Whaling Museum

known. Here are harpoons, lances, and the tools used in separating blubber from whale carcasses. A permanent exhibit, "Mark Well the Whale," details the history and impact of whaling on the locality. The museum features the state's only fully equipped nineteenth-century whaleboat with original gear; an extensive collection of the whaler's art of scrimshaw; and "The Wonder of Whales" conservation gallery for children.

The Whaling Museum, Box 25, Cold Spring Harbor 11724, (516) 367-3418, is open daily from Memorial Day through Labor Day; closed Monday during the rest of the year. Hours are 11:00 A.M. to 5:00 P.M. Admission is $2.00 for adults, $1.50 for senior citizens and children ages 6 to 12, and free for children 5 and under.

The ◆ **DNA Learing Center,** the educational arm of Cold Spring Harbor Laboratory, is the world's first biotechnology museum. Two- and three-dimensional displays, computer multimedia, videos, and other elements are utilized to teach visitors about genes. The newest exhibit, "Story of a Gene," is a comprehensive presentation on the biochemistry, physiology, medical uses, and social aspects of the human growth hormone (HGH)—all, we're assured, written and geared to a level appropriate for bright elementary students. The center also airs "Long Island Discovery," a twenty-eight-minute multimedia presentation exploring the history and heritage of Long Island.

DNA Learning Center, 334 Main Street, Cold Spring Harbor 11724, (516) 367-6808, is open weekdays 10:00 A.M. to 4:00 P.M. Call for film times and weekend and holiday hours. Admission is free.

The **Village Blacksmith** is a family enterprise launched in 1977 by Bernard and Ann Reichert and their sons, James and William. Not many families start up blacksmith shops anymore, but the Reicherts did it up right. They purchased an 1830 farmhouse that had served as a gas station, installed a forge, and set up shop selling handcrafted ironware made on the premises as well as items such as cast-iron and pewter reproductions. The output of the Reichert forge includes fireplace tools, trivets, chandeliers, sconces, hooks—just about every sort of useful wrought iron-ware, some of it commissioned by the smithy's clientele as custom work.

The Village Blacksmith, 141 Main Street, Northport 11768, (516) 757-3620, is open Monday through Saturday from 10:00 A.M. to 5:30 P.M. and Sunday, 11:00 A.M. to 5:00 P.M.

Don't miss a visit to the National Landmark **St. James General Store,** 516 Moriches Road, St. James, (516) 862-8333. In business since 1857, it's the oldest operating general store in the country and looks just as it did in 1890. More than four thousand nine-teenth-century-style items, including handmade quilts, salt glaze pottery, hand-carved decoys, penny candy, exotic teas, and bonnets, fill the store's venerable shelves. The store is open daily from 10:00 A.M. to 5:00 P.M.

The village of **Stony Brook,** on Long Island Sound, has it all: a scenic location, a fascinating history, great food and lodgings, museums, and terrific shopping. And it owes its present-day success primarily to one man, Ward Melville, whose vision helped the rural village to successfully metamorphose into a suburban center while still retaining its historic integrity. His plan, unveiled to the community in 1939, called for relocating businesses and homes so as to open the view to the harbor. The shops were moved to a "shopping center" at the head of the village green, and today more than forty of the trendiest shops on Long Island are housed at the **Stony Brook Village Center.** Up the road, the **Three Village Garden Club Exchange** features two floors of antiques and collectibles.

Stony Brook's **Three Village Inn,** built in 1751, was until 1867 the home of Captain Jonas Smith, Long Island's first millionaire/sea captain. Today it's a charming inn and restaurant, featuring homemade breads and desserts and house specialties such as cold plum soup, pan-roasted chicken breast stuffed with ham and Monterey Jack cheese, baked lobster pie, and, every Sunday, a "Thanksgiving" turkey dinner with all the trimmings. To make a room or meal reservation (breakfast, lunch, dinner, and Sunday brunch), call (516) 751–0555.

Within walking distance of the inn, at 1208 Route 25A, is **The Museums at Stony Brook,** a museum complex housing the **Margaret Melville Blackwell History Museum,** featuring American decor in miniature in a gallery of fifteen period rooms and one of the country's finest collections of antique decoys, plus a new exhibition, every two or three months, on a historical theme; the **Dorothy and Ward Melville Carriage House,** with its world-renowned collection of more than ninety horse-drawn carriages; and the **Art Museum,** exhibiting American art from the eighteenth century to the present, as well as collected works of American genre painter William Sidney Mount (1807–1868). There are also a **1794 barn,** an **1867 carriage shed,** an **1875 blacksmith shop,** and an **1877 one-room schoolhouse.** The museums are open year-round, Wednesday through Saturday and on Monday and holidays, 10.00 A.M. to 5:00 P.M. and Sunday, noon to 5:00 P.M. Closed Thanksgiving Day, December 24 and 25, and New Year's Day. Admission is $4.00 for adults; $3.00 for seniors, and $2.00 for students from elementary school through college. For information call (516) 751-0066.

A "must see" before leaving town is the working **Gristmill** on Harbor Road, built circa 1751 and renovated through the efforts of Mr. Melville in 1947. It's open Wednesday through Friday, 11:00 A.M. to 4:30 P.M. and Saturday and Sunday, noon to 4:30 P.M. Admission is $1.00 for adults; children under 12, 50 cents. For information call (516) 751-2244.

More than ninety-five tanks and artillery pieces from the Civil War through Operation Desert Storm are displayed at ◆ **American Armoured Foundation, Inc. (A.A.F.),** which has one of the country's largest collections of tanks and ordnance. The museum also displays a large assemblage of machine guns, rocket launchers, flame throwers, mortars, and rifles as well as cavalry helmets, uniforms. and military memorabilia.

A.A.F., 2383 Fifth Avenue, Ronkonkoma 11779, (516) 588-0033, is open May through October, Wednesday through Sunday, 11:00 A.M. to 4:00 P.M. and November through April, Sunday only from 11:00 A.M. to 4:00 P.M. Admission is $5.00 for adults and

$4.00 for children 5 to 12 and senior citizens. Children 4 and under are free.

Like Planting Fields in Oyster Bay, the south shore's ◆ **Bayard Cutting Arboretum** is another rich man's estate that has become a mecca for those who enjoy majestic trees and beautiful gardens. The arboretum, which is virtually adjacent to the state-managed Connetquot River State Park Preserve, was once the property of one of New York City's ablest financiers. William Bayard Cutting (1850–1912) was a lawyer, railroad director and president, banker, insurance executive, and philanthropist, noted for having built the first block of Manhattan tenements to feature indoor plumbing.

In his leisure time (whenever that might have been), Cutting enjoyed himself by improving his Long Island retreat. He built the sixty-eight-room Tudor mansion that stands on the arboretum grounds in 1886, with a few decorative touches by his friend Louis Comfort Tiffany. (Visitors can enter the mansion, the former dining room of which houses a well-maintained collection of mounted birds.) When it came to landscaping, Cutting placed a good deal of trust in another friend, the great Harvard botanist and silviculturist Charles Sprague Sargent. Together with none other than Frederick Law Olmsted, Sargent was responsible for much of the appearance of the Cutting estate and, subsequently, the arboretum.

The Bayard Cutting Arboretum is an especially pleasant place for a quiet stroll, even for those not well versed in tree species. Azaleas and rhododendrons grow here in profusion. The streams and ponds, with their ducks and geese and graceful little footbridges, are reason enough to spend an afternoon at the Cutting.

The Bayard Cutting Arboretum, Route 27A, Oakdale 11769, (516) 581-1002, is open Tuesday through Sunday, 10:00 A.M. to sunset. Admission is $4.00 per car; free from November through March.

Within a few miles of the Bayard Cutting Arboretum, on the Great South Bay that divides the barrier beach of Fire Island from the Long Island mainland, is the village of West Sayville, with its **Long Island Maritime Museum.** The whalers of Cold Spring Harbor were by no means the only brave Long Islanders to go down to the sea in ships to pursue their quarry; here in West Sayville, men went out into dangerous waters to harvest the more prosaic but nonetheless important oyster. The maritime museum, in fact, includes a vintage 1907 restored oyster house and has among its holdings the largest collection of small craft on Long Island. There is also a restored boat-builder's shop, illustrative of the skill and care that went into the buildings of these essential commercial vessels. Other exhibits concentrate upon the tools of oystermen over the years.

It isn't all oysters at the Long Island Maritime Museum. Displays of yachting and racing memorabilia, model boats, and artifacts related to the lifesaving service of the nineteenth century round out the museum's collection. Duck and other shorebird decoys, an integral part of American folk art in shoreline communities well into this century, are also on exhibit. The Bayman's Cottage depicts the style of living at the turn of the century.

Long Island Maritime Museum, Route 27A, West Sayville 11796, (516) 854-4974, is open Wednesday through Saturday, 10:00 A.M. to 3:00 P.M. and Sunday, noon to 4:00 P.M. Admission is free, but donations are appreciated.

Elsie Collins's ❖ **1880 House** is a delightful, antique-filled B & B just a few blocks from Westhampton Beach. There are two large suites, each with its own adjoining sitting room and private bath in the farmhouse, and a third in an adjacent 100-year-old barn. Guests can cool off in the swimming pool after a game of tennis or warm up by the fireplace after a brisk winter's walk on the beach. The B & B, at Two Seafield Lane, Westhampton Beach 11978, (516) 288-1559 or (800) 346-3290, is open year-round. Rates, including breakfast, range from $100 per day off season to $200 per day weekends in season. There's a two-day minimum stay in season.

At ❖ **Slo Jack's Miniature Golf,** Long Island's oldest, the windmill has been turning since 1960. It's the miniature course of our dreams, complete with a wishing well, paddle wheels, and a sixties drive-in restaurant (car service no longer offered) that serves up hamburgers, hot dogs, soft-serve ice cream, Mexican food, and local seafood. Official season at Slo Jack's Miniature Golf, 212 West Montauk Highway, Hampton Bay 11946, (516) 728-9601, is Memorial Day to Labor Day, but the restaurant is open all year, and unofficially the course is open mid-March until Christmas. Both are open 10:00 A.M. to 11:00 P.M.

If you're looking for peace and quiet, beautiful beaches, or simply a taste of island life, take a short ferry ride to **Shelter Island,** cradled between the North and South forks of Long Island. The car ferries leave from Greenport on the North Fork and North Haven on the South Shore. The Nature Conservancy owns nearly one-third of the 8,000-acre island, assuring that this portion, at least, will remain unspoiled. There are four trails on the Conservancy's **Mashomack Preserve** for nature study and bird-watching, varying in length from 1.5 miles to 11 miles, and a barrier-free Braille trail for the visually impaired. In the village you can rent bicycles at **Piccozzi's Bike Shop** (516–749–0045), sip a frozen drink on the waterfront patio at **Alfred's Place, Ltd.** (516–749–3355), grab a bite at **Chamberlain's** (516–749–2005), have a lovely meal at the Victorian **Chequit Inn** (516–749–0018), or stop in at one of the other restaurants. By now you'll have fallen in love with the island and vowed never to leave. There are plenty of places to put up. The Chequit Inn also has guest rooms, as do a number of other places, including the **Beech Tree House** (516–749–4252), which has suites with full kitchens, and **Shelter Island Resort,** overlooking Shelter Island Sound (516–749–2001). For more information contact the Shelter Island Chamber of Commerce, Box 598, Shelter Island 11964, (516) 749–0399.

INDEX

ABOUT THE AUTHORS

William G. and Kay Scheller are co-authors of *New Jersey: Off the Beaten Path* and contributors to several National Geographic books, including *Crossing America* and *Scenic Byways*. In addition they are co-authors of the New England volume in the series of driving guides for the United States, also published by National Geographic. Their work has appeared in several Fodor's publications and in guidebook publications of *Yankee Magazine*.